THE GLAD TIDINGS OF BAHÁ'U'LLÁH

By the Same Author

CHRIST AND BAHÁ'U'LLÁH
THE HEART OF THE GOSPEL
THE MISSION OF BAHÁ'U'LLÁH
THE PROMISE OF ALL AGES

The Glad Tidings of Bahá'u'lláh

Being extracts from the Sacred Writings of the Bahá'ís

With Introduction and Notes by
GEORGE TOWNSHEND, M.A.

GEORGE RONALD
OXFORD

GEORGE RONALD PUBLISHERS
46 High Street, Kidlington, Oxford OX5 2DN

This book was originally published in 1949 by
John Murray (Publishers) Ltd
in *The Wisdom of the East* series

This Revised Edition 1975
Reprinted 1978

COPYRIGHT 1949 BY GEORGE TOWNSHEND
Bibliography, Notes and Revisions
© George Ronald 1975

ISBN 0 85398 045 4 Paper
ISBN 0 85398 046 2 Cased

EXTRACTS FROM THE FOLLOWING WORKS
REPRINTED BY PERMISSION:

By Bahá'u'lláh: *Gleanings from the Writings of Bahá'u'lláh*, Copyright © 1939, 1952 by the National Spiritual Assembly of the Bahá'ís of the United States; *Prayers and Meditations*, Copyright © 1938 by the National Spiritual Assembly of the Bahá'ís of the United States; *The Kitáb-i-Íqán: The Book of Certitude*, 2nd ed., Copyright © 1931, 1950 by the National Spiritual Assembly of the Bahá'ís of the United States; *The Seven Valleys and the Four Valleys*, 2nd rev. ed., Copyright © 1945, 1952, 1975 by the National Spiritual Assembly of the Bahá'ís of the United States. By 'Abdu'l-Bahá: *Some Answered Questions*, rev. ed., Copyright © 1930, 1954, 1964 by the National Spiritual Assembly of the Bahá'ís of the United States. By Shoghi Effendi: *The World Order of Bahá'u'lláh: Selected Letters*, 2nd rev. ed., Copyright © 1938, 1955, 1974; *The Promised Day Is Come*, rev. ed., Copyright © 1941, 1961; *The Advent of Divine Justice*, 3rd rev. ed., Copyright © 1939, 1963, 1966 by the National Spiritual Assembly of the Bahá'ís of the United States. By Nabíl-i-A'ẓam [Muḥammad-i-Zarandí]: *The Dawn-Breakers: Nabíl's Narrative of the Early Days of the Bahá'í Revelation*, Copyright © 1932 by the National Spiritual Assembly of the Bahá'ís of the United States.

Printed in Great Britain by
Fletcher & Son Ltd, Norwich

CONTENTS

		PAGE
INTRODUCTION	. . . .	1
CHAPTER I.	BUILDING THE WORLD ANEW	11
CHAPTER II.	GOD'S COMMAND AND EXHORTATION . .	52
CHAPTER III.	THE PROCLAMATION OF THE DAY OF GOD .	70
CHAPTER IV.	THE JOURNEY OF THE SOUL	81
BIBLIOGRAPHY	. . . .	111
REFERENCES	. . . .	113

EDITORIAL NOTE TO THE 1975 REVISED EDITION

It has long been regretted by Bahá'ís in many different countries that this selection of Bahá'í Scripture, originally published by John Murray in the Wisdom of the East series, has been unavailable for a number of years. The selection was compiled by the late Hand of the Cause George Townshend, sometime Canon of St. Patrick's Cathedral, Dublin, and Archdeacon of Clonfert. It is a wide-ranging one, useful to the student, the traveller, the lecturer, the teacher, or indeed to anyone who wants a convenient resumé, in the words of Scripture, of the tenets of the Bahá'í Faith. In addition there are Mr. Townshend's inspiring notes and introduction.

This edition is essentially a photographic reproduction of the original 1949 edition. Very little has been changed. There are some typographical corrections, in two cases older translations have been replaced with later ones by Shoghi Effendi, and new Bibliography and References have been added. The introduction is unchanged.

The Bahá'í Faith has expanded rapidly since 1949, at first under the guidance of Shoghi Effendi, the Guardian of the Faith from 1921 until his death in 1957. Since 1963, the Universal House of Justice, the supreme elective body instituted by Bahá'u'lláh, has directed the affairs of the world-wide Bahá'í community. The statistics mentioned by George Townshend in his introduction have long been out of date. At April 1975, the chief statistics were as follows:

National Spiritual Assemblies	119
Centres and Communities	72,000
Countries opened to the Faith	330
Languages into which Bahá'í literature has been translated	546

INTRODUCTION

The Central Figures of the Bahá'í Faith

The Forerunner: *The Báb* (The Gate)   1819–1850
The Founder: *Bahá'u'lláh* (The Glory of God)   1817–1892
The Expounder: *'Abdu'l-Bahá* (The Servant of the Glory)   1844–1921

All the selections in this volume are from the words of the Báb, Bahá'u'lláh, or 'Abdu'l-Bahá.

The present Guardian of the Cause, and spiritual head of the Bahá'í World-Community is Shoghi Effendi, grandson of 'Abdu'l-Bahá.

The Purpose of the Faith

The primary mission of the Faith is to enable every adherent of an earlier World-Faith to obtain a fuller understanding of the religion with which he stands identified and to acquire a clear apprehension of its purpose.

The supreme mission of the Faith is the achievement of the organic and spiritual unity of the whole body of the nations, which will involve the emergence of a world-community, the consciousness of world-citizenship and the founding of a world civilization and culture.

*   *   *   *   *   *   *

The message of Bahá'u'lláh is a message of victory and power, a message of light shining in a darkness that comprehended it not and scattering that darkness for ever, of God's wiping away all tears from men's eyes, of the lone star of Faith guiding mankind out of the night to a day that needs no sun to light it, for it is lit by the glory of God himself.

This hour ere we pass out of the midmost gloom of that awful cataclysm which the Bahá'í Prophet more than seventy years ago so unerringly foretold, this hour when perplexity follows upon perplexity and no way out of chaos seems to open and men's hearts still fail them for fear, this is the hour when mankind needs and has a right to hear the divine message of comfort, of forgiveness after judgment, the promise of a glory that shall shine for ever, of a day that shall be followed by no night.

" To-day . . . the call of the Kingdom is heard in all lands and the breath of the Holy Spirit is felt in all hearts that are faithful. . . . This is a new cycle of human power. All the horizons of the world are luminous and the world will become indeed as a garden and a paradise. It is the hour of the unity of the sons of men and of the drawing together of all races and all classes. You are loosed from ancient superstitions which have kept men ignorant, destroying the foundations of true humanity.

" The gift of God to this enlightened age is the knowledge of the oneness of mankind and the fundamental oneness of religion. War shall cease between nations and by the will of God the Most Great Peace shall come ; the world will be seen as a new world and all men will live as brothers. . . ."

So spake 'Abdu'l-Bahá when, not long after the first book of Bahá'í writings had appeared in this Series (*The Splendour of God*, 1909), he came himself to our shores bringing the message of Bahá'u'lláh.

At the close of his visit, seeing that in spite of the warm and wonderful welcome given him, the world in general did not appreciate the spiritual opportunities of the time ; he gave his message in the form of a challenge and of a call to action, and as he departed for the East left ringing in men's ears the Reveille of the Day of God.

> Glad Tidings!
> The doors of the Kingdom of God are open!
> Glad Tidings!
> Armies of angels are descending from heaven!
> Glad Tidings!
> The Sun of Truth is rising . . .
> Glad Tidings!
> The Trumpet is sounding;
> Glad Tidings!
> The Banner of the Most Great Peace
> is floating far and wide . . . .
> Glad Tidings!
> The Holy Spirit is being outpoured.
> Glad Tidings!
> For everlasting life is here.
> O ye that sleep, awake!
> O ye heedless ones, learn wisdom.
> O blind, receive your sight!
> O deaf, hear!
> O dumb, speak!
> O dead, arise!
> Be happy!
> Be happy!
> Be full of joy.

In these few simple sentences 'Abdu'l-Bahá gives the spirit and substance of the Bahá'í Message: a message which in an age laden with darkness and foreboding opens the vision of a golden future for mankind and summons men to venture all they have and all they are in a final assault upon the Gates of Hell and in the establishment at last of the Kingdom of Heaven upon the earth.

It tells—this celestial message—of immeasurable bounties poured forth at the feet of mankind by the generosity of God;

it tells of glorious attainments, never before within human reach, that wait close at hand for realization in this maturing age. It proclaims that the Prophetic Cycle is closed: the Cycle of Fulfilment is here. The bible promises have come true. This is the day wherein mankind will find through recognition of God's presence and submission to his command the deliverance and the peace which it has hitherto sought in vain.

From the tragic story of the life of Bahá'u'lláh and of the ruthless persecution of him and of his followers it would seem as though the oppressors of the earth and all the forces of evil knew instinctively how dire was the threat to their ancient dominion over mankind, and put forth against him the utmost effort of their concerted strength. After the martyrdom of his herald, the Báb, the government and the priesthood of his country opposed him. His possessions were confiscated. His relatives and friends were killed. He was thrown into a dungeon; was four times exiled; and was finally imprisoned in 'Akká where he spent twenty-four years. His enemies were kings, despots against whom with their armies and their fifty million subjects Bahá'u'lláh stood through all his ministry singly and alone.

"Yet these great numbers," it is written, "instead of being able to dominate him could not withstand his wonderful personality and the power and the influence of his heavenly cause. Although they were determined upon extinguishing the light in that most brilliant lantern, yet they were ultimately defeated and overthrown, and day by day his splendour became more radiant. They made every effort to lessen his greatness, but his prestige grew in proportion to their efforts to diminish it. Surrounded by enemies who were seeking his life, he never sought to conceal himself, did nothing to protect himself: on the contrary in his spiritual might and power he was at all times

INTRODUCTION

visible before the faces of men, easy of access, serenely withstanding the multitudes who were opposing him."

Had he not been endowed with more than mortal courage, had he not drawn upon hidden springs of celestial strength, he never could have borne down the forces of enemies so many and so mighty. Had not his Word brought light and comfort and sweetness to men and women, helping them to solve the problems of life and to meet their difficulties, it never could have been so precious that thousands would choose to die rather than renounce it, nor could it have made headway against the prejudice and apathy of an unbelieving world.

At first slowly, precariously, in the face of acute danger, the Faith spread its message and its blessings. In the lifetime of its Herald, the Báb, it reached Persia and 'Iráq. In that of Bahá'u'lláh it reached—in spite of proscription—ten other lands of the Near and Middle East, travelling as far as India and Burma. Between 1892 and 1921, the period of 'Abdu'l-Bahá's ministry, it was carried to the Far East, to China and Japan, to Europe, to Australia and South Africa, to the Far West, to the United States and Brazil, to the Hawaii Islands : entering, in all, thirty-two countries. Since then it has gone far and wide over the globe at a steadily increasing speed and has continually deepened its influence on the hearts and minds of thoughtful men and women.

It has now entered ninety-one countries. Its literature is translated and printed in fifty-one languages. It has enrolled in its world-community representatives of thirty-one races. It has established contact with numerous minority groups : with Cherokee Indians in North Carolina, with Eskimos in Alaska, with Inca Indians in Peru, with Laps in Scandinavia, with Maoris in New Zealand, with Mayans in Yucatan, with Mexican Indians in Mexico, with Oneida Indians in Wisconsin, with Patagonian Indians in Argentina. Eighty-eight of its Assemblies, national and local, have been incorporated. Bahá'ís are domiciled in more than thirty localities in Australasia, more than forty in Germany and Austria, more than sixty in Canada, than eighty in India and Burma, than one hundred in Latin America, than seven hundred in Persia and in upwards of twelve hundred localities in the United States.

International Bahá'í Congresses held in South and Central America and an inter-European Teaching Conference in Geneva pave the way for a World-Bahá'í Congress. Recognition extended to the Faith by the United Nations as an international non-governmental body has permitted the appointment of accredited representatives to United Nations Conferences.

The vigour, the speed, the enthusiasm, the success of its missionary work has been paralleled by the growth of a varied and world-wide literature. It includes translations of historical and philosophical works on the Faith by distinguished apostles of Bahá'u'lláh; commentaries, textbooks and treatises by western writers; a large biennial international record, fully illustrated, of Bahá'í activities; as well as magazines, newsletters, journals and the like, produced in many lands and often circulated through the globe, all revolving around the central and basic writings of the Faith—the Sacred Word of Bahá'u'lláh and of 'Abdu'l-Bahá together with the authoritative expositions given by the Guardian of the Cause. The majority of these central Writings now available in English have appeared since the first selection of Bahá'í writings was published in this Series forty years ago. The most important of these later publications are *The Epistle to the Son of the Wolf* by Bahá'u'lláh, *Gleanings* from his works, and a companion volume of devotional selections, entitled *Prayers and Meditations* (all of them masterpieces of translation by the Guardian, in which the eloquence of Bahá'u'lláh, which was likened to a rushing torrent, is rendered

INTRODUCTION 7

into powerful and vigorous English prose) : and *The Promulgation of Universal Peace*, by 'Abdu'l-Bahá, his Addresses given in London (1911) and in Paris (1912), three volumes of his *Tablets*, and lastly his "Will and Testament".

It is therefore much more possible than it was forty years ago for a reader to appreciate the distinctive purpose of the Faith, and to form a judgment on its timeliness and value. The following statement on its place in the succession of world-religions has recently been made by the Guardian.

"This Faith is now increasingly demonstrating its right to be recognized not as one more religious system superimposed on the conflicting creeds which for so many generations have divided mankind and darkened its fortunes, but rather as a restatement of the eternal verities underlying all the religions of the past, as a unifying force instilling into the adherents of these religions a new spiritual vigour, infusing them with a new hope and love for mankind, firing them with a new vision of the fundamental unity of their religious doctrines, and unfolding to their eyes the glorious destiny that awaits the human race.

"The fundamental principle enunciated by Bahá'u'lláh, the followers of His Faith firmly believe, is that religious truth is not absolute but relative, that Divine Revelation is a continuous and progressive process, that all the great religions of the world are divine in origin, that their basic principles are in complete harmony, that their aims and purposes are one and the same, that their teachings are but facets of one truth, that their functions are complementary, that they differ only in the non-essential aspects of their doctrines, and that their missions represent successive stages in the spiritual evolution of human society.

"The aim of Bahá'u'lláh, the Prophet of this new and great age which humanity has entered upon—He whose advent fulfils the prophecies of the Old and New Testaments as well as those of the Qur'án regarding the coming of the Promised One in the end of time, on the Day of Judgment—is not to destroy but to fulfil the Revelations of the past, to reconcile rather than accentuate the divergencies of the conflicting creeds which disrupt present-day society."

All the Prophets of the past came to mankind, as Bahá'u'lláh has done, with gifts of light and love and joy. They came in the hour of man's need, in a time of oppression, when love had grown cold and faith was dying, and men knew not good from evil. They came as deliverers, breathing new life into dead souls, transforming satanic defects into heavenly virtues. Each lifted his followers from degradation to glory, from ignorance to knowledge, from captivity to celestial freedom. They unveiled new visions, awakened magnanimities long disused, they summoned to lofty aims and high endeavour. Through them the love of God and the deep happiness, long forgotten, of sacrifice and surrender to his will were born again. Through them human nature became changed, ennobled: illusions vanished; fears died away, and with them, self-pity. They brought within human reach more gifts than man has ever yet shown readiness to accept. Pointing forward into a golden future, they promised mankind the bestowal of bounties richer yet and bade their followers watch with steadfast expectancy for one who should come to guide them yet further on their journey to the Kingdom.

But never yet had any Prophet brought a message so joyous, so triumphant as that of Bahá'u'lláh. Never yet had any declared the greatness of his Revelation in terms so transcendent as he.

"I testify before God", he proclaims, "to the greatness, the inconceivable greatness of this Revelation. Again and again have We in most of our Tablets borne witness to this truth that mankind may be roused from its heedlessness." And again:

"In this most mighty Revelation, all the Dispensations of the past have attained their highest, their final consummation." And again, "That which has been made manifest in this pre-eminent, this most exalted Revelation stands unparalleled in the annals of the past nor will future ages witness its like."

"The Hand of Omnipotence", he writes elsewhere, "hath established His Revelation upon an unassailable . . . foundation. Storms of human strife are powerless to undermine its basis nor will men's fanciful theories succeed in damaging its structure."

Terrible to-day is the plight of man as he lies sunk in unbelief, in defiance of divine law, in degradation, in hardness of heart, looking from a dreadful past into a dark future and wondering what doom of destruction it may hold for him and all the race.

But Bahá'u'lláh who long ago foresaw and foretold these wars and tribulations, proclaimed that God's love was greater than his wrath, that his mercy would outreach his judgment. He who came to earth to seek his lost children would seek until he found. Man's heart would be changed and cleansed; his darkened eyes would be opened, he would behold his God, and be saved.

In the parable of the Good Shepherd seeking the sheep that was lost, in the parable of the Prodigal at last coming to himself and returning to his Father, Jesus told in moving words of the regeneration of the human soul, of the reunion of man's heart with the heart of his Creator.

Regeneration is likewise the central theme and aim of the Faith of Bahá'u'lláh.

But the regeneration now in view is not that of an individual only, nor of any multitude of individuals. It is that of humanity as a whole, as a single spiritual organism, as one soul in many bodies.

Unregenerate mankind is to-day a grievous case. But the end is not yet.

The end of Christ's story was the lamb held in the loving

Shepherd's arms, the Father running to meet his son and falling on his neck and calling to his servants—" Bring forth the best robe and put it on him. And put a ring on his hand, and shoes on his feet. For this my son was dead and is alive again : he was lost and is found."

And the end of the story of to-day, though it be yet in the distance, is a race forgiven, rescued and redeemed, radiant with happiness, looking back at the horror of its Day of Judgment only that it may with deeper gratitude praise the deliverer who came bringing regeneration and eternal life.

" All created things ", said Bahá'u'lláh, " proclaim the evidences of this world-wide regeneration. . . . This is the most great, the most joyful tidings imparted by the pen of this wronged One to mankind."

The Sacred Writings of the Bahá'í Faith are numerous and cover all aspects of human life. Nearly twenty volumes have already been published in an English version and many other pieces are to be found in Bahá'í pamphlets and periodicals or as citations in the works of Shoghi Effendi. The aim of this book is to develop a single distinctive idea throughout. The following extracts have been chosen to set forth in brief compass but in long perspective the master-purpose of the mission of Bahá'u'lláh : the achievement of the spiritual and organic unification of mankind and the establishment of a world-civilization. They show the pattern of the future for which the Bahá'ís are working and the deeply conceived plan of reconstruction which the Prophet called the nations to undertake in a universal co-ordinated effort. The emphasis of the selections is rather on the ethical than the administrative phase of the Bahá'í Teaching, and the final chapter carries the world-problem back into the human heart and presents it as being ultimately spiritual and personal.

CHAPTER I

BUILDING THE WORLD ANEW

Bahá'u'lláh received his call to Prophethood in Ṭihrán, Persia, in the year 1853. He made his public declaration of this call in Ba<u>gh</u>dád in 1863. He passed away in 'Akká, Palestine, in 1892, having been an exile and a prisoner of the Sulṭán and the <u>Sh</u>áh for nearly forty years.

Among his chief prophetic words are " The Hidden Words ", " The Seven Valleys ", " The Book of Certitude ", written before his Declaration; the various Tablets to the Kings written approximately from 1865 to 1869, and His Most Holy Book, published a few years later.

In his teaching Bahá'u'lláh affirmed that God in this Age has again interposed in human affairs and that at his command the invisible celestial forces which rule and overrule the course of history and the destiny of nations are set unalterably towards the building of a peaceful and permanent world-commonwealth. No opposition by man will be suffered to frustrate the glorious purpose of the Father; nor will any man-made method of reconstruction succeed,—but only the divinely designed system which (it is the mission of Bahá'u'lláh to reveal) sets forth the plan and pattern of a new world made after the desire of God.

He appeals to monarchs, governments and religious leaders as well as to the peoples, to recognize that the present constitution of human society must be modified in order that it may correspond with the development of mankind and the requirements of the New Age.

Two things he teaches are now essential for the well being of the nations: first, a consciousness of world citizenship; second, the emergence of a world-community.

The oneness of mankind is to be the paramount principle in world-reconstruction ; and national processes everywhere have to be readjusted to conform to this.

" It is not for him to pride himself who loveth his own country but rather for him who loveth the whole world. The earth is but one country and mankind its citizens." *And again he wrote,* " That one indeed is a man who to-day dedicateth himself to the service of the entire human race." *Religion would be the foundation of the entire structure, for, he wrote,* " Religion is the greatest of all means for the establishment of order in the world and for the peaceful contentment of all that dwell therein."

A 1. The world's equilibrium hath been upset through the vibrating influence of this most great, this new World Order. Mankind's ordered life hath been revolutionized through the agency of this unique, this wondrous System—the like of which mortal eyes have never witnessed.

Immerse yourselves in the ocean of My words, that ye may unravel its secrets, and discover all the pearls of wisdom that lie hid in its depths. Take heed that ye do not vacillate in your determination to embrace the truth of this Cause—a Cause through which the potentialities of the might of God have been revealed, and His sovereignty established. With faces beaming with joy, hasten ye unto Him. This is the changeless Faith of God, eternal in the past, eternal in the future. Let him that seeketh, attain it ; and as to him that hath refused to seek it—verily, God is Self-Sufficient, above any need of His creatures.

Say : This is the infallible Balance which the Hand of God is holding, in which all who are in the heavens and all who are on the earth are weighed, and their fate determined, if ye be of them that believe and recognize this truth. Say : Through it the poor have been enriched, the learned enlightened, and the seekers enabled to ascend unto the presence of God. Beware, lest ye make it a cause of dissension amongst you. Be ye as firmly settled as the immovable mountain in the Cause of your Lord, the Mighty, the Loving.

[*Gleanings from the Writings of Bahá'u'lláh*]

A 2. The All-Knowing Physician hath His finger on the pulse of mankind. He perceiveth the disease, and prescribeth, in His unerring wisdom, the remedy. Every age hath its own problem, and every soul its particular aspiration. The remedy the world needeth in its present-day afflictions can never be the same as that which a subsequent age may require. Be anxiously concerned with the needs of the age ye live in, and centre your deliberations on its exigencies and requirements.

We can well perceive how the whole human race is encompassed with great, with incalculable afflictions. We see it languishing on its bed of sickness, sore-tried and disillusioned. They that are intoxicated by self-conceit have interposed themselves between it and the Divine and infallible Physician. Witness how they have entangled all men, themselves included, in the mesh of their devices. They can neither discover the cause of the disease, nor have they any knowledge of the remedy. They have conceived the straight to be crooked, and have imagined their friend an enemy.

Incline your ears to the sweet melody of this Prisoner. Arise, and lift up your voices, that haply they that are fast asleep may be awakened. Say: O ye who are as dead! The Hand of Divine bounty proffereth unto you the Water of Life. Hasten and drink your fill. Whoso hath been re-born in this Day, shall never die; whoso remaineth dead, shall never live.

[*Gleanings from the Writings of Bahá'u'lláh*]

A 3. Behold the disturbances which, for many a long year, have afflicted the earth, and the perturbation that hath seized its peoples. It hath either been ravaged by war, or tormented by sudden and unforeseen calamities. Though the world is encompassed with misery and distress, yet no man hath paused to reflect what the cause or source of that may be. Whenever the True Counsellor uttered a word in admonishment, lo, they all denounced Him as a mover of mischief and rejected His claim. How bewildering, how confusing is such behaviour! No two men can be found who may be said to be outwardly and inwardly united. The evidences of discord and malice are apparent everywhere, though all were made for harmony and union. The Great Being saith: O well-beloved ones! The tabernacle of unity hath been raised; regard ye not one another as strangers. Ye are the fruits of one tree, and the leaves of one branch. We cherish the hope that the light of justice may shine upon the world and sanctify it from tyranny. If the rulers and kings of the earth, the symbols of the power of God, exalted be His glory, arise and resolve to dedicate themselves to whatever will promote the highest interests of the whole of humanity, the reign of justice will assuredly be established amongst the children of men, and the effulgence of its light will envelop the whole earth. The Great Being saith: The structure of world stability and order hath been reared upon, and will continue to be sustained by, the twin pillars of reward and punishment. . . . In another passage He hath written: Take heed, O concourse of the rulers of the world! There is no force on earth that can equal in its conquering power the force of justice and wisdom. . . . Blessed is the king who marcheth with the ensign of wisdom unfurled before him, and the battalions of justice massed in his rear. He verily is the ornament that adorneth the brow of peace and the countenance of security. There can be no doubt whatever that if the day star of justice, which the clouds of tyranny have obscured, were to shed its light upon men, the face of the earth would be completely transformed.

[*Gleanings from the Writings of Bahá'u'lláh*]

In the later sixties of the nineteenth century Bahá'u'lláh proclaimed his Mission in a series of letters to the kings of the earth. One of these was addressed to all the kings of the East and West collectively; others to individual monarchs. The two following passages are taken from his letter to Queen Victoria.

A 4. O ye rulers of the earth! Wherefore have ye clouded the radiance of the Sun, and caused it to cease from shining? Hearken unto the counsel given you by the Pen of the Most High, that haply both ye and the poor may attain unto tranquillity and peace. We beseech God to assist the kings of the earth to establish peace on earth. He, verily, doth what He willeth.

O kings of the earth! We see you increasing every year your expenditures, and laying the burden thereof on your subjects. This, verily, is wholly and grossly unjust. Fear the sighs and tears of this Wronged One, and lay not excessive burdens on your peoples. Do not rob them to rear palaces for yourselves; nay rather choose for them that which ye choose for yourselves. Thus We unfold to your eyes that which profiteth you, if ye but perceive. Your people are your treasures. Beware lest your rule violate the commandments of God, and ye deliver your wards to the hands of the robber. By them ye rule, by their means ye subsist, by their aid ye conquer. Yet, how disdainfully ye look upon them! How strange, how very strange!

Now that ye have refused the Most Great Peace, hold

ye fast unto this, the Lesser Peace, that haply ye may in some degree better your own condition and that of your dependents.

O rulers of the earth! Be reconciled among yourselves, that ye may need no more armaments save in a measure to safeguard your territories and dominions. Beware lest ye disregard the counsel of the All-Knowing, the Faithful.

Be united, O kings of the earth, for thereby will the tempest of discord be stilled amongst you, and your peoples find rest, if ye be of them that comprehend. Should any one among you take up arms against another, rise ye all against him, for this is naught but manifest justice.

[*Gleanings from the Writings of Bahá'u'lláh*]

A 5. O ye the elected representatives of the people in every land! Take ye counsel together, and let your concern be only for that which profiteth mankind, and bettereth the condition thereof, if ye be of them that scan heedfully.

Regard the world as the human body which, though at its creation whole and perfect, hath been afflicted, through various causes, with grave disorders and maladies. Not for one day did it gain ease, nay its sickness waxed more severe, as it fell under the treatment of ignorant physicians, who gave full rein to their personal desires, and have erred grievously. And if, at one time, through the care of an able physician, a member of that body was healed, the rest remained afflicted as before. Thus informeth you the All-Knowing, the All-Wise.

We behold it, in this day, at the mercy of rulers so drunk with pride that they cannot discern clearly their own best advantage, much less recognize a Revelation so bewildering and challenging as this. And whenever any one of them hath striven to improve its condition, his motive hath been his own gain, whether confessedly so or not; and the unworthiness of this motive hath limited his power to heal or cure.

That which the Lord hath ordained as the sovereign remedy and mightiest instrument for the healing of all the world is the union of all its peoples in one universal Cause, one common Faith. This can in no wise be achieved except through the power of a skilled, an all-powerful and inspired Physician. This, verily, is the truth, and all else naught but error.

[*Gleanings from the Writings of Bahá'u'lláh*]

A 6. He Who is your Lord, the All-Merciful, cherisheth in His heart the desire of beholding the entire human race as one soul and one body. Haste ye to win your share of God's good grace and mercy in this Day that eclipseth all other created Days. How great the felicity that awaiteth the man that forsaketh all he hath in a desire to obtain the things of God! Such a man, We testify, is among God's blessed ones.

[*Gleanings from the Writings of Bahá'u'lláh*]

A 7. O contending peoples and kindreds of the earth! Set your faces towards unity, and let the radiance of its light shine upon you. Gather ye together, and for the sake of God resolve to root out whatever is the source of contention amongst you. Then will the effulgence of the world's great Luminary envelop the whole earth, and its inhabitants become the citizens of one city, and the occupants of one and the same throne. This wronged One hath, ever since the early days of His life, cherished none other desire but this, and will continue to entertain no wish except this wish. There can be no doubt whatever that the peoples of the world, of whatever race or religion, derive their inspiration from one heavenly Source, and are the subjects of one God. The difference between the ordinances under which they abide should be attributed to the varying requirements and exigencies of the age in which they were revealed. All of them, except a few which are the outcome of human perversity, were ordained of God, and are a reflection of His Will and Purpose. Arise and, armed with the power of faith, shatter to pieces the gods of your vain imaginings, the sowers of dissension amongst you. Cleave unto that which draweth you together and uniteth you. This, verily, is the most exalted Word which the Mother Book hath sent down and revealed unto you. To this beareth witness the Tongue of Grandeur from His habitation of glory.

[*Gleanings from the Writings of Bahá'u'lláh*]

A 8. The Great Being saith : O ye children of men ! The fundamental purpose animating the Faith of God and His Religion is to safeguard the interests and promote the unity of the human race, and to foster the spirit of love and fellowship amongst men. Suffer it not to become a source of dissension and discord, of hate and enmity. This is the straight Path, the fixed and immovable foundation. Whatsoever is raised on this foundation, the changes and chances of the world can never impair its strength, nor will the revolution of countless centuries undermine its structure. Our hope is that the world's religious leaders and the rulers thereof will unitedly arise for the reformation of this age and the rehabilitation of its fortunes. Let them, after meditating on its needs, take counsel together and, through anxious and full deliberation, administer to a diseased and sorely-afflicted world the remedy it requires. . . . It is incumbent upon them who are in authority to exercise moderation in all things. Whatsoever passeth beyond the limits of moderation will cease to exert a beneficial influence. Consider for instance such things as liberty, civilization and the like. However much men of understanding may favourably regard them, they will, if carried to excess, exercise a pernicious influence upon men. ... Please God, the peoples of the world may be led, as the result of the high endeavours exerted by their rulers and the wise and learned amongst men, to recognize their best interests. How long will humanity persist in its waywardness? How long will injustice continue? How long is chaos and confusion to reign amongst men? How long will discord agitate the face of society? The winds of despair are, alas, blowing from every direction, and the strife that divideth and afflicteth the human race is daily increasing. The signs of impending convulsions and chaos can now be discerned, inasmuch as the prevailing order appeareth to be lamentably defective. I beseech God, exalted be His glory, that He may graciously awaken the peoples of the earth, may grant that the end of their conduct may be profitable unto them, and aid them to accomplish that which beseemeth their station.

[*Gleanings from the Writings of Bahá'u'lláh*]

A 9. The Great Being, wishing to reveal the prerequisites of the peace and tranquillity of the world and the advancement of its peoples, hath written: The time must come when the imperative necessity for the holding of a vast, an all-embracing assemblage of men will be universally realized. The rulers and kings of the earth must needs attend it, and, participating in its deliberations, must consider such ways and means as will lay the foundations of the world's Great Peace amongst men. Such a peace demandeth that the Great Powers should resolve, for the sake of the tranquillity of the peoples of the earth, to be fully reconciled among themselves. Should any king take up arms against another, all should unitedly arise and prevent him. If this be done, the nations of the world will no longer require any armaments, except for the purpose of preserving the security of their realms and of maintaining internal order within their territories. This will ensure the peace and composure of every people, government and nation. We fain would hope that the kings and rulers of the earth, the mirrors of the gracious and almighty name of God, may attain unto this station, and shield mankind from the onslaught of tyranny.

. . . The day is approaching when all the peoples of the world will have adopted one universal language and one common script. When this is achieved, to whatsoever city a man may journey, it shall be as if he were entering his own home. These things are obligatory and absolutely essential. It is incumbent upon every man of insight and understanding to strive to translate that which hath been written into reality and action. . . . That one indeed is a man who, to-day, dedicateth himself to the service of the entire human race. The Great Being saith: Blessed and happy is he that ariseth to promote the best interests of the peoples and kindreds of the earth. In another passage He hath proclaimed: It is not for him to pride himself who loveth his own country, but rather for him who loveth the whole world. The earth is but one country, and mankind its citizens.

[*Gleanings from the Writings of Bahá'u'lláh*]

'Abdu'l-Bahá expounded with great simplicity, charm and force, with clearness and with fullness, the principles and the plans which Bahá'u'lláh had revealed for mankind's attainment of " The Most Great Peace " and for the creation thereafter of a divine civilization. These comprehensive expositions are contained in many " Tablets " or letters, in his work " Secrets of Divine Civilization " published in 1882 in Bombay and in 1957 in Wilmette (in an English version); in his Addresses delivered in London (1911), in Paris (1911), and more especially in those delivered in America (1912) which have been

published in two volumes bearing the title he gave them, " The Promulgation of Universal Peace ".

B 1. The divine manifestations since the day of Adam have striven to unite humanity so that all may be accounted as one soul. The function and purpose of a shepherd is to gather and not disperse his flock. The prophets of God have been divine shepherds of humanity. They have established a bond of love and unity among mankind, made scattered peoples one nation and wandering tribes a mighty kingdom. They have laid the foundation of the oneness of God and summoned all to Universal Peace. All these holy, divine manifestations are one. They have served one God, promulgated the same truth, founded the same institutions and reflected the same light. Their appearances have been successive and correlated ; each one has announced and extolled the one who was to follow and all laid the foundation of reality. They summoned and invited the people to love and made the human world a mirror of the Word of God. Therefore the divine religions they established have one foundation ; their teachings, proofs and evidences are one ; in name and form they differ but in reality they agree and are the same. These holy manifestations have been as the coming of springtime in the world. Although the Springtime of this year is designated by another name according to the changing calendar, yet as regards its life and quickening it is the same as the springtime of last year. For each spring is the time of a new creation, the effects, bestowals, perfections and life-giving forces of which are the same as those of the former vernal seasons although the names are many and various. This is 1912, last year's was 1911, and so on, but in fundamental reality no difference is apparent. The sun is one but the dawning-points of the sun are numerous and changing. The ocean is one body of water but different parts of it have particular designation, Atlantic, Pacific, Mediterranean, Antarctic, etc. If we consider the names, there is differentiation, but the water, the ocean itself is one reality.

Likewise the divine religions of the holy manifestations of God are in reality one, though in name and nomenclature they differ.

. . . The strife between religions, nations and races arises from misunderstanding. If we investigate the religions to discover the principles underlying their foundations we will find they agree, for the fundamental reality of them is one and not multiple. By this means the religionists of the world will reach their point of unity and reconciliation. They will ascertain the truth that the purpose of religion is the acquisition of praise-worthy virtues, betterment of morals, spiritual development of mankind, the real life and divine bestowals. All the prophets have been the promoters of these principles; none of them has been the promoter of corruption, vice or evil. They have summoned mankind to all good. They have united people in the love of God, invited them to the religions of the unity of mankind and exhorted them to amity and agreement. For example, we mention Abraham and Moses. By this mention we do not mean the limitation implied in the mere names but intend the virtues which these names embody. When we say "Abraham" we mean thereby a manifestation of divine guidance, a centre of human virtues, a source of heavenly bestowals to mankind, a dawning-point of divine inspiration and perfections. These perfections and graces are not limited to names and boundaries. When we find these virtues, qualities and attributes in any personality, we recognize the same reality shining from within and bow in acknowledgment of the Abrahamic perfections. Similarly we acknowledge and adore the beauty of Moses. Some souls were lovers of the name

Abraham, loving the lantern instead of the light and when they saw this same light shining from another lantern they were so attached to the former lantern that they did not recognize its later appearance and illumination. Therefore those who were attached and held tenaciously to the name Abraham were deprived when the Abrahamic virtues reappeared in Moses. Similarly the Jews were believers in His Holiness Moses, awaiting the coming of the Messiah. The virtues and perfections of Moses became apparent in His Holiness Jesus Christ most effulgently but the Jews held to the name Moses, not adoring the virtues and perfections manifest in him. Had they been adoring these virtues and seeking these perfections they would assuredly have believed in His Holiness Jesus Christ when the same virtues and perfections shone in him. If we are lovers of the light we adore it in whatever lamp it may become manifest, but if we love the lamp itself and the light is transferred to another lamp we will neither accept nor sanction it. Therefore we must follow and adore the virtues revealed in the messengers of God whether in Abraham, Moses, Jesus or other prophets, but we must not adhere to and adore the lamp. We must recognize the sun no matter from what dawning-point it may shine forth, be it Mosaic, Abrahamic or any personal point of orientation whatever, for we are lovers of sunlight and not of orientation. We are lovers of illumination and not of lamps and candles. We are seekers for water no matter from what rock it may gush forth. We are in need of fruit in whatsoever orchard it may be ripened. We long for rain, it matters not which cloud pours it down. We must not be fettered. If we renounce these fetters we shall agree, for all are seekers of reality. The counterfeit or imitation of true religion has adulterated human belief and the foundations have been lost sight of. The variance of these imitations has produced enmity and strife, war and bloodshed.

Now the glorious and brilliant twentieth century has dawned and the divine bounty is radiating universally. The Sun of Truth is shining forth in intense enkindlement. This is verily the century when these imitations must be forsaken, superstitions abandoned and God alone worshipped. We must look at the reality of the prophets and their teachings in order that we may agree.

[*The Promulgation of Universal Peace*]

B 2. His Holiness Bahá'u'lláh the Sun of Truth has dawned from the horizon of the Orient, flooding all regions with the light and life which will never pass away....

Every one who truly seeks and justly reflects will admit that the teachings of the present day emanating from mere human sources and authority are the cause of difficulty and disagreement amongst mankind, the very destroyers of humanity whereas the teachings of Bahá'u'lláh are the very healing of the sick world, the remedy for every need and condition. In them may be found the realization of every desire and aspiration, the cause of the happiness of the world of humanity, the stimulus and illumination of mentality, the impulse for advancement and uplift, the basis of unity for all nations, the fountain-source of love amongst mankind, the centre of agreement, the means of peace and harmony, the one bond which will unite the east and the west.

After every night there is a morn. In the supreme wisdom of God it is decreed that when the gross darkness of religious hatred and hostility, the obscurity of religious ignorance, superstition and blind imitations cover the world, the Sun of Truth shall arise and the spirit of reality become manifest and reflected in human hearts. At such a time as this Bahá'u'lláh appeared upon the horizon of the Orient. For fifty years he endured the greatest hardships and ordeals, ever striving to dispel the darkness of religious conditions, to remove the cause of enmity and rancour, to awaken the world of humanity from the beds of negligence and heedlessness by the flashing light of the glorious glad-tidings and trumpet-tone of the heavenly call and summons. For the spread of this message he offered his life and bore every vicissitude. He passed fifty years in prison, chains and exile. He was always under the threat and menace of the sword, yet he uplifted the standard of divine teachings and flooded the world of the east with illumination. In the Orient to-day the light of the heavenly glad-tidings is visible everywhere, the divine call is heard, the effulgence of the Sun of Reality is shining, the precious rain is down-pouring from the clouds of mercy, and the breaths of the Holy Spirit are bestowing fresh life upon the hearts of men. Ere long the darkness will pass away entirely and the regions of the east will become completely illumined; enmity, hatred, ignorance and bigotry will no longer remain; the satanic powers which destroy human equality and religious unity will be dethroned and the nations will dwell in peace and harmony under the overspreading banner of the oneness of humanity. Therefore we supplicate the Lord our God with sincere and contrite hearts asking aid and assistance in the accomplishment of this mighty end; that the nations shall be unified in the Word of God; that war, enmity and hatred between races, religions, nativities and denominations shall disappear and be forever unknown; and that peoples and nations shall spiritually embrace each other in the indissoluble bond and power of the love of God. Then will the world of humanity become radiant and the human race enjoy to the fullest capacity the graces of divine bestowal. So long as religious discord and enmity continue among mankind, the world of humanity will find neither happiness, rest nor composure.

Pray that God may assist in this heavenly undertaking, that the world of mankind shall be saved from the ordeals of ignorance, blindness and spiritual death. Then will you behold light upon light, joy upon joy, absolute happiness reigning everywhere, the people of the religions consorting together in fragrance and felicity, this world in its maturity becoming the reflection of the eternal kingdom and this terrestrial abode of man the very paradise of God. Pray for this! Pray for this!

[*The Promulgation of Universal Peace*]

B 3. All created things have their degree or stage of maturity. The period of maturity in the life of a tree is the time of its fruit-bearing. The maturity of a plant is the time of its blossoming and flower. The animal attains a stage of full growth and completeness, and in the human kingdom man reaches his maturity when the lights of intelligence have their greatest power and development.

From the beginning to the end of his life man passes through certain periods or stages each of which is marked by certain conditions peculiar to itself. For instance during the period of childhood his conditions and requirements are characteristic of that degree of intelligence and capacity. After a time he enters the period of youth in which his former conditions and needs are superseded by new requirements applicable to the advance in his degree. His faculties of observation are broadened and deepened, his intelligent capacities are trained and awakened, the limitations and environment of childhood no longer restrict his energies and accomplishments. At last he passes out of the period of youth and enters the stage or station of maturity which necessitates another transformation and corresponding advance in his sphere of life-activity. New powers and perceptions clothe him, teaching and training commensurate with his progression occupy his mind, special bounties and bestowals descend in proportion to his increased capacities and his former period of youth and its conditions will no longer satisfy his matured view and vision.

Similarly there are periods and stages in the life of the aggregate world of humanity which at one time was passing through its degree of childhood, at another its time of youth, but now has entered its long presaged period of maturity, the evidences of which are everywhere visible and apparent. Therefore the requirements and conditions of former periods have changed and merged into exigencies which distinctly characterize the present age of the world of mankind. That which was applicable to human needs during the early history of the race could neither meet nor satisfy the demands of this day and period of newness and consummation. Humanity has emerged from its former degrees of limitation and preliminary training. Man must now become imbued with new virtues and powers, new moralities, new capacities. New bounties, bestowals and perfections are awaiting and already descending upon him. The gifts and graces of the period of youth although timely and sufficient during the adolescence of the world of mankind are now incapable of meeting the requirements of its maturity. The playthings of childhood and infancy no longer satisfy or interest the adult mind.

From every standpoint the world of humanity is undergoing a re-formation. The laws of former governments and civilizations are in process of revision, scientific ideas and theories are developing and advancing to meet a new range of phenomena, invention and discovery are penetrating hitherto unknown fields revealing new wonders and hidden secrets of the material universe ; industries have vastly wider scope and production ; everywhere the world of mankind is in the throes of evolutionary activity indicating the passing of the old conditions and advent of the new age of re-formation. Old trees yield no fruitage ; old ideas and methods are obsolete and worthless now. Old standards of ethics, moral codes and methods of living in the past will not suffice for the present age of advancement and progress.

This is the cycle of maturity and re-formation in religion as well. Dogmatic imitations of ancestral beliefs are passing. They have been the axis around which religion revolved but now are no longer fruitful ; on the contrary, in this day they have become the cause of human degradation and hindrance. Bigotry and dogmatic adherence to ancient beliefs have become the central and fundamental source of animosity among men, the obstacle to human progress, the cause of warfare and strife, the destroyer of peace, composure and welfare in the world. Consider conditions in the Balkans to-day ; fathers, mothers, children in grief and lamentation, the foundations of life overturned, cities laid waste and fertile lands made desolate by the ravages of war. These conditions are the outcome of hostility and hatred between nations and peoples of religion who imitate and adhere to the forms and violate the spirit and reality of the divine teachings.

While this is true and apparent, it is likewise evident that the Lord of mankind has bestowed infinite bounties upon the world in this century of maturity and consummation. The ocean of divine mercy is surging, the vernal showers are descending, the Sun of Reality is shining gloriously. Heavenly teachings applicable to the advancement in human conditions have been revealed in this merciful age. This re-formation and renewal of the fundamental reality of religion constitute the true and outworking spirit of modernism, the unmistakable light of the world, the manifest effulgence of the Word of God, the divine remedy for all human ailment and the bounty of eternal life to all mankind.

[*The Promulgation of Universal Peace*]

B 4. In cycles gone by, though harmony was established, yet, owing to the absence of means, the unity of all mankind could not have been achieved. Continents remained widely divided, nay even among the peoples of one and the same continent association and interchange of thought were well-nigh impossible. Consequently intercourse, understanding and unity amongst all the peoples and kindreds of the earth were unattainable. In this day, however, means of communication have multiplied, and the five continents of the earth have virtually merged into one. . . . In like manner all the members of the human family, whether peoples or governments, cities or villages, have become increasingly interdependent. For none is self-sufficiency any longer possible, inasmuch as political ties unite all peoples and nations, and the bonds of trade and industry, of agriculture and education, are being strengthened every day. Hence the unity of all mankind can in this day be achieved. Verily this is none other but one of the wonders of this wondrous age, this glorious century. Of this past ages have been deprived, for this century—the century of light—has been endowed with unique and unprecedented glory, power and illumination. Hence the miraculous unfolding of a fresh marvel every day. Eventually it will be seen how bright its candles will burn in the assemblage of man.

Behold how its light is now dawning upon the world's darkened horizon. The first candle is unity in the political realm, the early glimmerings of which can now be discerned. The second candle is unity of thought in world undertakings, the consummation of which will ere long be witnessed. The third candle is unity in freedom which will surely come to pass. The fourth candle is unity in religion which is the corner-stone of the foundation itself, and which, by the power of God, will be revealed in all its splendour. The fifth candle is the unity of nations—a unity which in this century will be securely established, causing all the peoples of the world to regard themselves as citizens of one common fatherland. The sixth candle is unity of races, making of all that dwell on earth peoples and kindreds of one race. The seventh candle is unity of language, i.e., the choice of a universal tongue in which all peoples will be instructed and converse. Each and every one of these will inevitably come to pass, inasmuch as the power of the Kingdom of God will aid and assist in their realization.

[*A Tablet of 'Abdu'l-Bahá*]

B 5. In order that human souls, minds and spirits may attain advancement, tranquillity and vision in broader horizons of unity and knowledge, His Holiness Bahá'u'lláh proclaimed certain principles or teachings, some of which I will mention.

First—Man must independently investigate the reality; for the disagreements and dissensions which afflict and affect humanity, primarily proceed from imitations of ancestral beliefs and adherences to hereditary forms of worship. These imitations are accidental and without sanction in the holy books. They are the outcomes of human interpretations and teachings which have arisen, gradually, obscuring the real light of divine meaning and causing men to differ and dissent. The reality proclaimed in the heavenly books and divine teachings is ever conducive to love, unity and fellowship.

Second—The oneness of the world of humanity shall be realized, accepted and established. When we reflect upon this blessed principle, it will become evident and manifest that it is the healing remedy for all human conditions. All mankind are the servants of the glorious God our creator. He has created all. Assuredly he must have loved them equally, otherwise he would not have created them. He protects all. Assuredly he loves his creatures, otherwise he would not protect them. He provides for all, proving his love for all without distinction or preference. He manifests his perfect goodness and loving kindness toward all. He does not punish us for our sins and shortcomings, and we are all immersed in the ocean of his infinite mercy. Inasmuch as God is clement and loving to his children, lenient and merciful toward our shortcomings, why should we be unkind and unforgiving toward each other? As he loves humanity without distinction or preference, why should we not love all? Can we conceive of a plan and policy superior to the divine purpose? Manifestly we cannot. Therefore we must strive to do the will of the glorious Lord and emulate his policy of loving all mankind. The wisdom and policy of God are reality and truth whereas human policy is accidental and limited to our finite understanding. The policy of God is infinite. We must emulate his example. If a soul be ailing and infirm we must produce remedies; if ignorant we must provide education; if defective we must train and perfect that which is lacking; if immature and undeveloped we must supply the means of attainment to maturity. No soul should be hated, none neglected; nay, rather, their very imperfections should demand greater kindness and tender compassion. Therefore if we follow the example of the Lord of divinity, we will love all mankind from our hearts; and the means of the unity of the world of humanity will become as evident and manifest to us as the light of the sun. And from our example, the light of the love of God will be enkindled among men. For God is love, and all phenomena find source and emanation in that divine current of creation. The love of God haloes all created things. Were it not for the love of God no animate being would exist. This is clear manifest vision and truth unless a man is veiled by superstitions and a captive to imaginations, differentiating mankind according to his own estimate, loving some and hating others. Such an attitude is most unworthy and ignoble.

Third—Religion must be the mainspring and source of love in the world; for religion is the revelation of the will of God, the divine fundamental of which is love. Therefore if religion should prove to be the cause of enmity and hatred instead of love, its absence is preferable to its existence.

Fourth—Religion must reconcile and be in harmony with science and reason. If the religious beliefs of mankind are contrary to science and opposed to reason, they are none other than superstitions and without divine authority; for the Lord God has endowed man with the faculty of reason in order that through its exercise he may arrive at the verities of existence. Reason is the discoverer of the realities of things; and that which conflicts with its conclusions is the product of human fancy and imagination.

Fifth—Prejudice whether it be religious, racial, patriotic or political in its origin and aspect is the destroyer of human foundations and opposed to the commands of God. God has sent forth his prophets for the sole purpose of creating love and unity in the world of human hearts. All the heavenly books are the written word of love. If they prove to be the cause of prejudice and human estrangement, they have become fruitless. Therefore religious prejudice is especially opposed to the will and command of God. Racial and national prejudice which separate mankind into groups and branches, likewise have a false and unjustifiable foundation, for all men are the children of Adam and essentially of one family. There should be no racial alienation or national division among humankind. Such distinctions as French, German, Persian, Anglo-Saxon are human and artificial; they have neither significance nor recognition in the estimation of God. In his estimate all are one, the children of one family; and God is equally kind to them. The earth has one surface. God has not divided this surface by boundaries and barriers to separate races and peoples. Man has set up and established these imaginary lines, giving to each restricted area a name and the limitation of a nativity or nationhood. By this division and separation into groups and branches of mankind, prejudice is engendered which becomes a fruitful source of war and strife. Impelled by this prejudice races and nations declare war against each other; the blood of the innocent is poured out and the earth torn by violence. Therefore it has been decreed by God in this day that these prejudices and differences shall be laid aside. All are commanded to seek the good pleasure of the Lord of unity, to follow his command and obey his will; in this way the world of humanity shall become illumined with the reality of love and reconciliation.

Sixth—The world of humanity is in need of the confirmations of the Holy Spirit. If man does not become the recipient of the heavenly bestowals and spiritual bounties, he remains in the plane and kingdom of the animal. For the distinction between the animal and man is that man is endowed with the potentiality of divinity in his nature whereas the animal is entirely bereft of that gift and attainment. Therefore if a man is bereft of the intuitive breathings of the Holy Spirit, deprived of divine bestowals, out of touch with the heavenly world and negligent of the eternal truths, though in image and likeness he is human, in reality he is an animal; even as His Holiness Christ declared " That which is born of flesh is flesh, and that which is born of the spirit is spirit." This means that if man be a captive of physical susceptibilities and be minus the quickening of spiritual emotions, he is merely an animal. But every soul who possesses spiritual susceptibilities and has attained a goodly portion of the bestowals of the Holy Spirit is alive with the divine life of the higher kingdom. The soul that is portionless and bereft is as dead. Therefore he says " Let the dead bury the dead." Just as the physical body of man is in need of its force of life, even so the human soul is in need of the divine animus and vivification emanating from the Holy Spirit. Without this vivification and sustenance, man would be an animal; nay, rather, dead.

Seventh—The necessity of education for all mankind is evident. Children especially must be trained and taught. If the parent cannot afford to do this owing to lack of means, the body politic must make necessary provision for its accomplishment. Through the broadening spirit of education, illiteracy will disappear and misunderstandings due to ignorance will pass away.

Eighth—Universal Peace will be established among the nations of the world by international agreement. The greatest catastrophe in the world of humanity to-day is war. Europe is a storehouse of explosives awaiting a spark. All the European nations are on edge, and a single flame will set on fire the whole of that continent. Implements of war and death are multiplied and increased to an inconceivable degree and the burden of military maintenance is taxing the various countries beyond the point of endurance. Armies and navies devour the substance and possessions of the people; the toiling poor, the innocent and helpless are forced by taxation to provide munitions and armament for governments bent upon conquest of territory and defence against powerful rival nations. There is no greater or more woeful ordeal in the world of humanity to-day than impending war. Therefore international peace is a crucial necessity. An arbitral court of justice shall be established by which international disputes are to be settled. Through this means all possibility of discord and war between the nations will be obviated.

Ninth—There must be an equality of rights between men and women. Women shall receive an equal privilege of education. This will enable them to qualify and progress in all degrees of occupation and accomplishment. For the world of humanity possesses two wings—man and woman. If one wing remains incapable and defective, it will restrict the power of the other, and full flight will be impossible. Therefore the completeness and perfection of the human world is dependent upon the equal development of these two factors.

Tenth—There shall be an equality of rights and prerogatives for all mankind.

Eleventh—One language must be selected as an international medium of speech and communication. Through this means misunderstandings will be lessened, fellowship established and unity assured.

These are a few of the principles proclaimed by His Holiness Bahá'u'lláh. He has provided the remedy for the ailments which now afflict the human world, solved the difficult problems of individual, social, national and universal welfare, and laid the foundation of divine reality upon which material and spiritual civilization are to be founded throughout the centuries before us.

[*The Promulgation of Universal Peace*]

B 6. One of Bahá'u'lláh's teachings is the adjustment of means of livelihood in human society. Under this adjustment there can be no extremes in human conditions as regards wealth and sustenance. For the community needs financier, farmer, merchant and labourer just as an army must be composed of commander, officers and privates. All cannot be commanders ; all cannot be officers or privates. Each in his station in the social fabric must be competent ; each in his function according to ability ; but justness of opportunity for all.

... Difference of capacity in human individuals is fundamental. It is impossible for all to be alike, all to be equal, all to be wise. Bahá'u'lláh has revealed principles and laws which will accomplish the adjustment of varying human capacities. He has said that whatsoever is possible of accomplishment in human government will be effected through these principles. When the laws he has instituted are carried out there will be no millionaires possible in the community and likewise no extremely poor. This will be effected and regulated by adjusting the different degrees of human capacity. The fundamental basis of the community is agriculture, tillage of the soil. All must be producers. Each person in the community whose income is equal to his individual producing capacity shall be exempt from taxation. But if his income is greater than his needs he must pay a tax until an adjustment is effected. That is to say, a man's capacity for production and his needs will be equalized and reconciled through taxation. If his production exceeds he will pay a tax; if his necessities exceed his production he shall receive an amount sufficient to equalize or adjust. Therefore taxation will be proportionate to capacity and production and there will be no poor in the community.

Bahá'u'lláh likewise commanded the rich to give freely to the poor. In the Kitab-el-Akdas it is further written by him that those who have a certain amount of income must give one-fifth of it to God the creator of heaven and earth.

[*The Promulgation of Universal Peace*]

B 7. The Bahá'í cause covers all economic and social questions under the heading and ruling of its laws. The essence of the Bahá'í spirit is that in order to establish a better social order and economic condition, there must be allegiance to the laws and principles of government. Under the laws which are to govern the world, the socialists may justly demand human rights but without resort to force and violence. The governments will enact these laws, establishing just legislation and economics in order that all humanity may enjoy full measure of welfare and privilege ; but this will always be according to legal protection and procedure. Without legislative administration, rights and demands fail and the welfare of the commonwealth cannot be realized. To-day the method of demand is the strike and resort to force which is manifestly wrong and destructive of human foundations. Rightful privilege and demand must be set forth in laws and regulations.

While thousands are considering these questions, we have more essential purposes. The fundamentals of the whole economic conditions are divine in nature and are associated with the world of the heart and spirit. This is fully explained in the Bahá'í teaching, and without knowledge of its principles no improvement in the economic state can be realized. The Bahá'ís will bring about this improvement and betterment, but not through sedition and appeal to physical force ; not through warfare, but welfare. Hearts must be so cemented together, love must become so dominant that the rich shall most willingly extend assistance to the poor and take steps to establish these economic adjustments permanently. If it is accomplished in this way it will be most praiseworthy because then it will be for the sake of God and in the pathway of his service. For example it will be as if the rich inhabitants of a city should say " It is neither just nor lawful that we should possess great wealth while there is abject poverty in this community," and then willingly give their wealth to the poor, retaining only as much as will enable them to live comfortably.

Strive therefore to create love in the hearts in order that they may become glowing and radiant. When that love is shining, it will permeate other hearts even as this electric light illumines its surroundings. When the love of God is established, everything else will be realized. This is the true foundation of all economics. . . .

[*The Promulgation of Universal Peace*]

B 8. True civilization will unfurl its banner in the midmost heart of the world whenever a certain number of its distinguished and high-minded sovereigns—the shining exemplars of devotion and determination—shall, for the good and happiness of all mankind, arise, with firm resolve and clear vision, to establish the Cause of Universal Peace. They must make the Cause of Peace the object of general consultation, and seek by every means in their power to establish a Union of the nations of the world. They must conclude a binding treaty and establish a covenant, the provisions of which shall be sound, inviolable and definite. They must proclaim it to all the world and obtain for it the sanction of all the human race. This supreme and noble undertaking—the real source of the peace and well-being of all the world—should be regarded as sacred by all that dwell on earth. All the forces of humanity must be mobilized to ensure the stability and permanence of this Most Great Covenant. In this all-embracing Pact the limits and frontiers of each and every nation should be clearly fixed, the principles underlying the relations of governments towards one another definitely laid down, and all international agreements and obligations ascertained. In like manner, the size of the armaments of every government should be strictly limited, for if the preparations for war and the military forces of any nation should be allowed to increase, they will arouse the suspicion of others. The fundamental principle underlying this solemn Pact should be so fixed that if any government later violate any one of its provisions, all the governments on earth should arise to reduce it to utter submission, nay the human race as a whole should resolve, with every power at its disposal, to destroy that government. Should this greatest of all remedies be applied to the sick body of the world, it will assuredly recover from its ills and will remain eternally safe and secure. . . .

A few, unaware of the power latent in human endeavour, consider this matter as highly impracticable, nay even beyond the scope of man's utmost efforts. Such is not the case, however. On the contrary, thanks to the unfailing grace of God, the loving-kindness of His favoured ones, the unrivalled endeavours of wise and capable souls, and the thoughts and ideas of the peerless leaders of this age, nothing whatsoever can be regarded as unattainable. Endeavour, ceaseless endeavour, is required. Nothing short of an indomitable determination can possibly achieve it. Many a cause which past ages have regarded as purely visionary, yet in this day has become most easy and practicable. Why should this most great and lofty Cause—the day-star of the firmament of true civilization and the cause of the glory, the advancement, the well-being and the success of all humanity—be regarded as impossible of achievement? Surely the day will come when its beauteous light shall shed illumination upon the assemblage of man.

[*The Secret of Divine Civilization*]

B 9. For example, the question of Universal Peace, about which His Holiness Bahá'u'lláh says that the *Supreme Tribunal* must be established : although the *League of Nations* has been brought into existence, yet it is incapable of establishing Universal Peace. But the Supreme Tribunal which His Holiness Bahá'u'lláh has described will fulfil this sacred task with the utmost might and power. And his plan is this: that the national assemblies of each country and nation—that is to say, their parliaments—should elect two or three persons who are the choicest men of that nation, and are well informed concerning international laws and the relations between governments and aware of the essential needs of the world of humanity in this day. The number of these representatives should be in proportion to the number of inhabitants of that country. The election of these souls who are chosen by the national assembly, that is, the parliament, must be confirmed by the upper house, the congress and the cabinet and also by the president or monarch so these persons may be the elected ones of all the nation and the government. From among these people the members of the Supreme Tribunal will be elected, and all mankind will thus have a share therein, for every one of these delegates is fully representative of his nation. When the Supreme Tribunal gives a ruling on any international question, either unanimously or by majority rule, there will no longer be any pretext for the plaintiff or ground of objection for the defendant. In case any of the governments or nations, in the execution of the irrefutable decision of the Supreme Tribunal, be negligent or dilatory, the rest of the nations will rise up against it, because all the governments and nations of the world are the supporters of this Supreme Tribunal. Consider what a firm foundation this is! But by a limited and restricted *League* the purpose will not be realized as it ought and should. This is the truth about the situation which has been stated ...

                [*Letter written to the Central Organization for a Durable Peace, The Hague, December 17, 1919*]

'Abdu'l-Bahá exhorts the people of the West to give ear to the Glad Tidings of the New Day, to recognize the urgency of the call

and to be true in their lives to the lofty principles enjoined by Bahá'u'lláh. He makes plain to them how far Christendom and all mankind have sunk below the level of their religious professions, and presses upon believers the duty of making known the Cause of God everywhere with all speed.

C 1. O Army of Life! East and West have joined to worship stars of faded splendour, and have turned in prayer unto darkened horizons. Both have utterly neglected the broad foundation of God's sacred laws, and have grown unmindful of the merits and virtues of His religion. They have regarded certain customs and conventions as the basis of the Divine faith, and have firmly established themselves therein. They have imagined themselves as having attained a glorious pinnacle of achievement and prosperity, when in reality they have touched the innermost depths of heedlessness and deprived themselves wholly of God's bounteous gifts.

The cornerstone of the religion of God is the acquisition of divine perfections and the sharing in His manifold bestowals. The essential purpose of faith and belief is to ennoble the inner being of man with the outpourings of grace from on high. If this be not attained, it is, indeed, deprivation. It is the realization of this deprivation that is the true eternal fire.

Therefore, it is incumbent upon all Bahá'ís to ponder this delicate and vital matter in their hearts, that, unlike other religions, they may not content themselves with the noise, the clamour, the hollowness of religious doctrine. Nay, rather, they should exemplify in every aspect of their lives the attributes and virtues that are born of God, and should arise to distinguish themselves by their goodly behaviour. They should justify their claim to be Bahá'ís by deeds, not by name.

He is a true Bahá'í who strives by day and by night to progress and advance along the path of human endeavour, whose cherished desire is so to live and act as to enrich and illumine the world ; whose source of inspiration is the Essence of Divine perfection ; whose aim in life is to conduct himself so as to be the cause of infinite progress. Only when he attains unto such perfect gifts can it be said of him that he is a Bahá'í.

In this holy dispensation, the crowning glory of bygone ages and cycles, faith is no mere acknowledgement of the unity of God, but rather the living of a life that manifests the virtues and perfections implied in such belief.

His Holiness the exalted One, may my life be a sacrifice to Him, has shown us the way of behaviour, has guided us to the path of self-sacrifice, has taught us how to despise earthly rest and comfort, and how to lay down our lives for each other. That sanctified Being, despite the loftiness of His position and the exaltation of His spirit, chose to be chained and fettered that we might obtain the light of divine guidance. All the days of His life He rested not for a moment. He sought no repose nor laid His head upon the couch of ease and security. His days were passed amid afflictions and suffering. How can we follow Him and yet remain idle and at ease ?

O my friends, arise to tend the pure and widely-scattered seed planted in the hearts of men. Dedicate yourselves wholly to the service of humanity. Then will the world be turned into a paradise ; then will the surface of the earth mirror forth the glory of the Abhá Kingdom. Should you fail in this, great will be your deprivation and grievous your loss.

O servant of truth, wouldst thou obtain the sovereignty of earth and heaven ? Seek nought but the true servitude upon the threshold of the Abhá Beauty. Wouldst thou win the joy of liberty in this world and the next ? Desire but submission unto His holy will. Wouldst thou discover the true way to God ?

Follow the path of His covenant. Wouldst thou behold the light of eternal splendour ? Fix thy gaze upon His bountiful grace vouchsafed from the Abhá Kingdom.

[*Bahá'í Scriptures* (British National Spiritual Assembly, 1941)]

C 2. I have repeatedly summoned you to the cause of the unity of the world of humanity, announcing that all mankind are the servants of the same God ; that God is the creator of all ; He is the provider and life-giver ; all are equally beloved by Him and are His servants upon whom His mercy and compassion descend. Therefore you must manifest the greatest kindness and love toward the nations of the world, setting aside fanaticism, abandoning religious, national and racial prejudice.

The earth is one nativity, one home, and all mankind are the children of one father. God has created them and they are the recipients of His compassion. Therefore if any one offends another, he offends God. It is the wish of our heavenly Father that every heart should rejoice and be filled with happiness ; that we should live together in felicity and joy. The obstacle to human happiness is racial or religious prejudice, the competitive struggle for existence and inhumanity toward each other.

Your eyes have been illumined, your ears are attentive, your hearts knowing. You must be free from prejudice and fanaticism, beholding no differences between the races and religions. You must look to God for He is the real shepherd and all humanity are His sheep. He loves them and loves them equally. As this is true, should the sheep quarrel among themselves ? They should manifest gratitude and thankfulness to God, and the best way to thank God is to love one another.

Beware lest ye offend any heart, lest ye speak against any one in His absence, lest ye estrange yourselves from the servants of

God. You must consider all His servants as your own family and relations. Direct your whole effort toward the happiness of those who are despondent, bestow food upon the hungry, clothe the needy and glorify the humble. Be a helper to every helpless one and manifest kindness to your fellow creatures in order that ye may attain the good-pleasure of God. This is conducive to the illumination of the world of humanity and eternal felicity for yourselves. I seek from God everlasting glory in your behalf; therefore this is my prayer and exhortation.

. . . —your efforts must be lofty. Exert yourselves with heart and soul so that perchance through your efforts the light of Universal Peace may shine and this darkness of estrangement and enmity may be dispelled from amongst men; that all men may become as one family and consort together in love and kindness; that the east may assist the west and the west give help to the east,—for all are the inhabitants of one planet, the people of one original nativity and the flocks of one shepherd.

Consider how the prophets who have been sent, the great souls who have appeared and the sages who have arisen in the world have exhorted mankind to unity and love. This has been the essence of their mission and teaching. This has been the goal of their guidance and message. The prophets, saints, seers and philosophers have sacrificed their lives in order to establish these principles and teachings amongst men. Consider the heedlessness of the world, for notwithstanding the efforts and sufferings of the prophets of God, the nations and peoples are still engaged in hostility and fighting. Notwithstanding the heavenly commandments to love one another, they are still shedding each other's blood. How heedless and ignorant are the people of the world! How gross the darkness which envelops them! Although they are the children of a compassionate God, they continue to live and act in opposition to His will and good-pleasure. God is loving and kind to all men, and yet they show the utmost enmity and hatred toward each other. God is the giver of life to them, and yet they constantly seek to destroy life. God blesses and protects their homes; they rage, sack and destroy each other's homes. Consider their ignorance and heedlessness!

Your duty is of another kind, for you are informed of the mysteries of God. Your eyes are illumined, your ears are quickened with hearing. You must therefore look toward each other and then toward mankind with the utmost love and kindness. You have no excuse to bring before God if you fail to live according to His command, for you are informed of that which constitutes the good-pleasure of God. You have heard His commandments and precepts. You must therefore be kind to all men; you must even treat your enemies as your friends. You must consider your evil-wishers as your well-wishers. Those who are not agreeable toward you must be regarded as those who are congenial and pleasant; so that perchance this darkness of disagreement and conflict may disappear from amongst men and the light of the divine may shine forth; so that the Orient may be illumined and the Occident filled with fragrance; nay, so that the east and west may embrace each other in love and deal with one another in sympathy and affection. Until man reaches this high station, the world of humanity shall not find rest, and eternal felicity shall not be attained. But if man lives up to these divine commandments, this world of earth shall be transformed into the world of heaven and this material sphere shall be converted into a paradise of glory. It is my hope that you may become successful in this high calling, so that like brilliant lamps you may cast light upon the world of humanity and quicken and stir the body of existence like unto a spirit of life. This is eternal glory. This is everlasting felicity. This is immortal life. This is heavenly attainment. This is being created in the image and likeness of God. And unto this I call you, praying to God to strengthen and bless you.

[*The Promulgation of Universal Peace*]

C 3. I hope that through the bounty and favours of the Most Glorious Lord, in this new age, the regions of the West become the East of the Sun of Truth, the believers of God become the dawning-places of lights, the manifestors of the signs, be protected and guarded from the doubts of the heedless ones, remain firm and steadfast in the Covenant and Testament, and strive day and night in order to awaken those who are asleep, to make mindful those who are heedless, to make confident of the mysteries of the Kingdom those who are deprived, to confer a share from the never-ending outpouring upon those who are helpless, to become the heralds of the Kingdom and to call the inhabitants of this terrestrial world to the Celestial Realm.

O ye Cohorts of God! To-day in the present world every community is wandering in a wilderness, follows the dictates of some passion and desire, and runs to and fro in pursuit of some imagination of its own. Among the communities of the world, this community of the " Most Great Name " is free from every such thought, keeping aloof from every such project and scheme, arising with the purest designs and intentions; it strives and endeavours with the utmost hope to live in accordance with the divine teachings in order that the surface of the earth become the delectable paradise, the nether world become the mirror of the Kingdom, the universe become another universe, and the human race attain to higher morals, conduct and manners.

O army of God! Through the protection and help vouchsafed by the Blessed Beauty—may my life be a sacrifice to His loved ones—ye must conduct yourselves in such a manner that ye may stand out distinguished and brilliant as the sun among other souls. Should any one of you enter a city, he should become a centre of attraction by reason of his sincerity, his faithfulness and love, his honesty and fidelity, his truthfulness and loving-kindness towards all the peoples of the world, so that the people of that city may cry out and say: "This man is unquestionably a Bahá'í, for his manners, his behaviour, his conduct, his morals, his nature, and disposition reflect the attributes of the Bahá'ís." Not until ye attain this station can ye be said to have been faithful to the Covenant and Testament of God. For according to the irrefutable texts, He has taken from us a firm covenant that we may live and act in accord with the divine exhortations, commands and lordly teachings.

O ye Cohorts of God! Now is the time when the signs and perfections of the "Most Great Name" become manifest and clear in this golden cycle in order that it may become demonstrated and established beyond doubt that this period is the period of the Blessed Perfection, and this cycle is distinguished from all other cycles and epochs.

O ye Cohorts of God! If you observe that a soul has turned his face completely toward the Cause of God, his intention is centralized upon the penetration of the Word of God, he is serving the Cause day and night with the utmost fidelity, no scent of selfishness is inhaled from his manners and deeds, and no trace of egotism or prejudice is seen in his personality—nay rather is he a wanderer in the wilderness of the love of God, and one intoxicated with the wine of the knowledge of God, occupied wholly with the diffusion of the fragrances of God, and attracted to the signs of the Kingdom of God; know ye of a certainty that he is confirmed with the powers of the Kingdom, assisted by the heaven of Might; and he will shine, gleam and sparkle like unto the morning star with the utmost brilliancy and splendour from the horizon of the everlasting gift. If he is alloyed with the slightest trace of passion, desire, ostentation or self-interest, it is certain that the results of all efforts will prove fruitless, and he will become deprived and hopeless.

O ye Cohorts of God ! Praise be to God !—that the Blessed Perfection hath freed men from the old bonds and fetters and released all from racial partisanship by proclaiming, " Ye are all the fruits of one tree and the leaves of one branch." Be ye kind to the human world, and be ye compassionate to the race of man, deal with the strangers as you deal with the friends, be ye gentle toward the outsiders as you are toward the beloved ones, know the enemy as the friend, look upon the satan as upon the angel, receive the unjust with the utmost love like unto a faithful one, and diffuse far and wide the fragrances of the musk of the gazelles of Kheta and Khotan to the nostrils of the ravenous wolves.

Become ye a shelter and asylum to the fearful ones, be ye a cause of tranquillity and ease to the souls and hearts of the agitated ones, impart ye strength to the helpless ones, become ye a treasury of wealth to the indigent ones, be ye a remedy and antidote to the afflicted ones, and a physician and nurse to the sick ones. Serve ye for the promotion of peace and concord and establish in this transitory world the foundation of friendship, fidelity, and reconciliation and truthfulness.

O ye Cohorts of God ! Strive ye that this human world may be changed into a luminous realm and this mound of earth become the Paradise of Abhá. Darkness hath environed the world upon all sides. Savage tempers and inclinations predominate. The human world has become the battlefield of the rapacious savages and the playground of the heedless and ignorant ones. The souls are either bloodthirsty wolves or beasts with degenerate reason. They are either deadly poison or worthless plants. There are a few souls who in reality have some humanitarian intentions and are thinking of the well-being and prosperity of human kind. You must in this instance (that is, service to humanity) sacrifice your lives, and in sacrificing your lives celebrate happiness and beatitude.

O ye Cohorts of God ! Beware lest ye offend the feelings of anyone, or sadden the heart of any person, or utter a reproach against anyone or censure him, whether he is a friend or stranger, believer or enemy. Pray in behalf of all and entreat God for forgiveness and bounty for all. Beware, beware of upbraiding or condemning a soul, though he may be an ill-wisher and an ill-doer. Do ye not look upon the creature, advance ye toward the Creator. Behold ye not the rebellious people, turn your faces toward the Lord of Hosts. Look ye not upon the ground, raise your eyes toward the world-illuminating Sun, which hath transformed every atom of the gloomy soil into bright and luminous substance.

O ye Cohorts of God ! In the moment of catastrophe, find ye patience, resignation and submission.

The more the calamities are intensified the less become ye disturbed. Withstand ye, with perfect assurance, the floods of trials and calamities, through the power of His Highness, the Almighty.
[*The Tablets of 'Abdu'l-Bahá*]

C 4. It is my desire that His Holiness Bahá'u'lláh shall be pleased with you ; that you may follow His precepts and become worthy of His confirmations. The requirements are that your minds must be illumined, your souls must be rejoiced with the glad tidings of God, you must become imbued with spiritual moralities, your daily life must evidence faith and assurance, your hearts must be sanctified and pure, reflecting a high degree of love and attraction toward the kingdom of El Abhá. You must become the lamps of Bahá'u'lláh so that you may shine with eternal light and be the proofs and evidences of His truth. Then will such signs of purity and chastity be witnessed in your deeds and actions that men will behold the heavenly radiance of your lives and say " Verily ye are the proofs of Bahá'u'lláh. Verily Bahá'u'lláh is the true one for He has trained such souls as these each one of whom is a proof in himself." They will say to others " Come and witness the conduct of these souls ; come and listen to their words, behold the illumination of their hearts, see the evidences of the love of God in them, consider their praiseworthy morals and discover the foundations of the oneness of humanity firmly implanted within them. What greater proof can there be than these people that the message of Bahá'u'lláh is Truth and Reality ? "

It is my hope that each one of you shall be a herald of God proclaiming the evidences of His appearance in words, deeds and thoughts. Let your actions and utterances be a witness that you are of the Kingdom of Bahá'u'lláh. These are the duties enjoined upon you by Bahá'u'lláh.

[*The Promulgation of Universal Peace*]

C 5. Now you must engage in the service of the Cause of God with the utmost firmness, steadfastness and resolution, and expend day and night in the promotion of the religion of God. Do not unloose your tongues save for conveying the Message ! Do not behold aught save the Kingdom of Abhá. Wish for no other companion save the true one. Do ye not desire other associates save turning thy face toward the Supreme Horizon. Do ye not search for any other delicacy save the Heavenly Food, and do ye not hope for any other sweetness save the love of the beauty of Abhá.

Spiritual means are prepared. The Merciful Table is spread and the banquet and the feast of the Lord is inexhaustible. Now is the time of attraction and ecstasy, so that that region may become wholly illumined and that worthless dust be changed into fragrant musk.

I declare by the Blessed Perfection (May my life be a sacrifice to His believers) that if the believers arise to act according to the good pleasure of the Blessed Perfection, the lights will be revealed, the mysteries discovered, the veils rent asunder, the darkness dispelled, the verses of unity chanted, and the melodies of the spiritual music of the glorious Lord sung.

Show ye an effort! Work unceasingly! labour diligently! so that the everlasting bounty be realized, eternal life be destined and the nostrils be perfumed with the holy fragrances.

[*A Tablet of 'Abdu'l-Bahá* (*Star of the West*, V, 1)]

CHAPTER II

GOD'S COMMAND AND EXHORTATION

The King of kings calls his vassals, the kings of the earth, and their subjects, and all the nations to the mightiest, most beneficent and glorious task ever undertaken in all the generations. He promises them that if they will arise at once with single-minded faith and enthusiasm God will bestow on them full support, and they will assuredly attain a victory and a dominion more illustrious and lasting than any which the Old Order of the world can offer them.

A 1. O kings of the earth ! He Who is the sovereign Lord of all is come. The Kingdom is God's, the omnipotent Protector, the Self-Subsisting. Worship none but God, and, with radiant hearts, lift up your faces unto your Lord, the Lord of all names. This is a Revelation to which whatever ye possess can never be compared, could ye but know it.

We see you rejoicing in that which ye have amassed for others and shutting out yourselves from the worlds which naught except My guarded Tablet can reckon. The treasures ye have laid up have drawn you far away from your ultimate objective. This ill beseemeth you, could ye but understand it. Wash from your hearts all earthly defilements, and hasten to enter the Kingdom of your Lord, the Creator of earth and heaven, Who caused the world to tremble and all its peoples to wail, except them that have renounced all things and clung to that which the Hidden Tablet hath ordained.

. . . Ye are but vassals, O kings of the earth ! He Who is the King of Kings hath appeared, arrayed in His most wondrous glory, and is summoning you unto Himself, the Help in Peril, the Self-Subsisting. Take heed lest pride deter you from recognizing the Source of Revelation, lest the things of this world shut you out as by a veil from Him Who is the Creator of heaven. Arise, and serve Him Who is the Desire of all nations, Who hath created you through a word from Him, and ordained you to be, for all time, the emblems of His sovereignty.

By the righteousness of God ! It is not Our wish to lay hands on your kingdoms. Our mission is to seize and possess the hearts of men. Upon them the eyes of Bahá are fastened. To this testifieth the Kingdom of Names, could ye but comprehend it. Whoso followeth his Lord, will renounce the world and all that is therein ; how much greater, then, must be the detachment of Him Who holdeth so august a station ! Forsake your palaces, and haste ye to gain admittance into His Kingdom. This, indeed, will profit you both in this world and in the next. To this testifieth the Lord of the realm on high, did ye but know it.

How great the blessedness that awaiteth the king who will arise to aid My Cause in My Kingdom, who will detach himself from all else but Me ! Such a king is numbered with the companions of the Crimson Ark—the Ark which God hath prepared for the people of Bahá. All must glorify his name, must reverence his station, and aid him to unlock the cities with the keys of My Name, the omnipotent Protector of all that inhabit the visible and invisible kingdoms. Such a king is the very eye of mankind, the luminous ornament on the brow of creation, the fountainhead of blessings unto the whole world. Offer up, O people of Bahá, your substance, nay your very lives, for his assistance.

[*Gleanings from the Writings of Bahá'u'lláh*]

A 2. A new life is, in this age, stirring within all the peoples of the earth ; and yet none hath discovered its cause or perceived its motive. Consider the peoples of the West. Witness how, in their pursuit of that which is vain and trivial, they have sacrificed, and are still sacrificing, countless lives for the sake of its establishment and promotion. The peoples of Persia, on the other hand, though the repository of a perspicuous and luminous Revelation, the glory of whose loftiness and renown hath encompassed the whole earth, are dispirited and sunk in deep lethargy.

O friends! Be not careless of the virtues with which ye have been endowed, neither be neglectful of your high destiny. Suffer not your labours to be wasted through the vain imaginations which certain hearts have devised. Ye are the stars of the heaven of understanding, the breeze that stirreth at the break of day, the soft-flowing waters upon which must depend the very life of all men, the letters inscribed upon His sacred scroll. With the utmost unity, and in a spirit of perfect fellowship, exert yourselves, that ye may be enabled to achieve that which beseemeth this Day of God. Verily I say, strife and dissension, and whatsoever the mind of man abhorreth are entirely unworthy of his station. Centre your energies in the propagation of the Faith of God. Whoso is worthy of so high a calling, let him arise and promote it. Whoso is unable, it is his duty to appoint him who will, in his stead, proclaim this Revelation, whose power hath caused the foundations of the mightiest structures to quake, every mountain to be crushed into dust, and every soul to be dumbfounded. Should the greatness of this Day be revealed in its fullness, every man would forsake a myriad lives in his longing to partake, though it be for one moment, of its great glory—how much more this world and its corruptible treasures!

Be ye guided by wisdom in all your doings, and cleave ye tenaciously unto it. Please God ye may all be strengthened to carry out that which is the Will of God, and may be graciously assisted to appreciate the rank conferred upon such of His loved ones as have arisen to serve Him and magnify His name. Upon them be the glory of God, the glory of all that is in the heavens and all that is on the earth, and the glory of the inmates of the most exalted Paradise, the heaven of heavens.

[*Gleanings from the Writings of Bahá'u'lláh*]

A 3. O Afnán, O thou that hast branched from Mine ancient Stock! My glory and My loving-kindness rest upon thee. How vast is the tabernacle of the Cause of God! It hath overshadowed all the peoples and kindreds of the earth, and will, ere long, gather together the whole of mankind beneath its shelter. Thy day of service is now come. Countless Tablets bear the testimony of the bounties vouchsafed unto thee. Arise for the triumph of My Cause, and, through the power of thine utterance, subdue the hearts of men. Thou must show forth that which will ensure the peace and the well-being of the miserable and the downtrodden. Gird up the loins of thine endeavour, that perchance thou mayest release the captive from his chains, and enable him to attain unto true liberty.

Justice is, in this day, bewailing its plight, and Equity groaneth beneath the yoke of oppression. The thick clouds of tyranny have darkened the face of the earth, and enveloped its peoples. Through the movement of Our Pen of glory We have, at the bidding of the omnipotent Ordainer, breathed a new life into every human frame, and instilled into every word a fresh potency. All created things proclaim the evidences of this world-wide regeneration. This is the most great, the most joyful tidings imparted by the pen of this wronged One to mankind. . . .

Every man of insight will, in this day, readily admit that the counsels which the Pen of this wronged One hath revealed constitute the supreme animating power for the advancement of the world and the exaltation of its peoples. Arise, O people, and, by the power of God's might, resolve to gain the victory over your own selves, that haply the whole earth may be freed and sanctified from its servitude to the gods of its idle fancies—gods that have inflicted such loss upon, and are responsible for the misery of, their wretched worshippers. These idols form the obstacle that impeded man in his efforts to advance in the path of perfection. We cherish the hope that the Hand of Divine power may lend its assistance to mankind, and deliver it from its state of grievous abasement.

[*Gleanings from the Writings of Bahá'u'lláh*]

A 4. O Kamál! The heights which, through the most gracious favour of God, mortal man can attain, in this Day, are as yet unrevealed to his sight. The world of being hath never had, nor doth it yet possess the capacity for such a revelation. The day, however, is approaching when the potentialities of so great a favour will, by virtue of His behest, be manifested unto men. Though the forces of the nations be arrayed against Him, though the kings of the earth be leagued to undermine His Cause, the power of His might shall stand unshaken. He, verily, speaketh the truth, and summoneth all mankind to the way of Him Who is the Incomparable, the All-Knowing.

All men have been created to carry forward an ever-advancing civilization. The Almighty beareth Me witness: To act like the beasts of the field is unworthy of man. Those virtues that befit his dignity are forbearance, mercy, compassion and loving-kindness toward all the peoples and kindreds of the earth. Say: O friends! Drink your fill from this crystal stream that floweth through the heavenly grace of Him Who is the Lord of Names. Let others partake of its waters in My name, that the leaders of men in every land may fully recognize the purpose for which the Eternal Truth hath been revealed, and the reason for which they themselves have been created.

[*Gleanings from the Writings of Bahá'u'lláh*]

A 5. Know thou that We have annulled the rule of the sword, as an aid to Our Cause, and substituted for it the power born of the utterance of men. Thus have We irrevocably decreed, by virtue of Our grace. Say: O people! Sow not the seeds of discord among men, and refrain from contending with your neighbour, for your Lord hath committed the world and the cities thereof to the care of the kings of the earth, and made them the emblems of His own power, by virtue of the sovereignty He hath chosen to bestow upon them. He hath refused to reserve for Himself any share whatever of this world's dominion. To this He Who is Himself the Eternal Truth will testify. The things He hath reserved for Himself are the cities of men's hearts, that He may cleanse them from all earthly defilements, and enable them to draw nigh unto the hallowed Spot which the hands of the infidel can never profane. Open, O people, the city of the human heart with the key of your utterance. Thus have We, according to a pre-ordained measure, prescribed unto you your duty.

By the righteousness of God! The world and its vanities, and its glory, and whatever delights it can offer, are all, in the sight of God, as worthless as, nay, even more contemptible than, dust and ashes. Would that the hearts of men could comprehend it! Wash yourselves thoroughly, O people of Bahá, from the defilement of the world, and of all that pertaineth unto it. God Himself beareth Me witness. The things of the earth ill beseem you. Cast them away unto such as may desire them, and fasten your eyes upon this most holy and effulgent Vision.

That which beseemeth you is the love of God, and the love of Him Who is the Manifestation of His Essence, and the observance of whatsoever He chooseth to prescribe unto you, did ye but know it.

Say: Let truthfulness and courtesy be your adorning. Suffer not yourselves to be deprived of the robe of forbearance and justice, that the sweet savours of holiness may be wafted from your hearts upon all created things. Say: Beware, O people of Bahá, lest ye walk in the ways of them whose words differ from their deeds. Strive that ye may be enabled to manifest to the peoples of the earth the signs of God, and to mirror forth His commandments. Let your acts be a guide unto all mankind, for the professions of most men, be they high or low, differ from their conduct. It is through your deeds that ye can distinguish yourselves from others. Through them the brightness of your light can be shed upon the whole earth. Happy is the man that heedeth My counsel, and keepeth the precepts prescribed by Him Who is the All-Knowing, the All-Wise.

[*Gleanings from the Writings of Bahá'u'lláh*]

A 6. The Most Great Name beareth Me witness! How sad if any man were, in this Day, to rest his heart on the transitory things of this world! Arise, and cling firmly to the Cause of God. Be most loving one to another. Burn away, wholly for the sake of the Well-Beloved, the veil of self with the flame of the undying Fire, and with faces joyous and beaming with light, associate with your neighbour. Ye have well observed, in all its aspects, the behaviour of Him Who is the Word of Truth amidst you. Ye know full well how hard it is for this Youth to allow, though it be for one night, the heart of any one of the beloved of God to be saddened by Him.

The Word of God hath set the heart of the world afire; how

regrettable if ye fail to be enkindled with its flame ! Please God, ye will regard this blessed night as the night of unity, will knit your souls together, and resolve to adorn yourselves with the ornament of a goodly and praiseworthy character. Let your principal concern be to rescue the fallen from the slough of impending extinction, and to help him embrace the ancient Faith of God. Your behaviour toward your neighbour should be such as to manifest clearly the signs of the one true God, for ye are the first among men to be re-created by His Spirit, the first to adore and bow the knee before Him, the first to circle round His throne of glory. I swear by Him Who hath caused Me to reveal whatever hath pleased Him ! Ye are better known to the inmates of the Kingdom on high than ye are known to your own selves. Think ye these words to be vain and empty ? Would that ye had the power to perceive the things your Lord, the All-Merciful, doth see—things that attest the excellence of your rank, that bear witness to the greatness of your worth, that proclaim the sublimity of your station ! God grant that your desires and unmortified passions may not hinder you from that which hath been ordained for you.

[*Gleanings from the Writings of Bahá'u'lláh*]

A 7. Release yourselves, O nightingales of God, from the thorns and brambles of wretchedness and misery, and wing your flight to the rose-garden of unfading splendour. O My friends that dwell upon the dust ! Haste forth unto your celestial habitation. Announce unto yourselves the joyful tidings : " He Who is the Best-Beloved is come ! He hath crowned Himself with the glory of God's Revelation, and hath unlocked to the face of men the doors of His ancient Paradise." Let all eyes rejoice, and let every ear be gladdened, for now is the time to gaze on His beauty, now is the fit time to hearken to His voice. Proclaim unto every longing lover : " Behold, your Well-Beloved hath come among men ! " and to the messengers of the Monarch of love impart the tidings : " Lo, the Adored One hath appeared arrayed in the fullness of His glory ! " O lovers of His beauty ! Turn the anguish of your separation from Him into the joy of an everlasting reunion, and let the sweetness of His presence dissolve the bitterness of your remoteness from His court.

Behold how the manifold grace of God, which is being showered from the clouds of Divine glory, hath, in this day, encompassed the world. For whereas in days past every lover besought and searched after his Beloved, it is the Beloved Himself Who is now calling His lovers and is inviting them to attain His presence. Take heed lest ye forfeit so precious a favour ; beware lest ye belittle so remarkable a token of His grace. Abandon not the incorruptible benefits, and be not content with that which perisheth. Lift up the veil that obscureth your vision, and dispel the darkness with which it is enveloped, that ye may gaze on the naked beauty of the Beloved's face, may behold that which no eye hath beheld, and hear that which no ear hath heard.

Hear Me, ye mortal birds ! In the Rose Garden of changeless splendour a Flower hath begun to bloom, compared to which every other flower is but a thorn, and before the brightness of Whose glory the very essence of beauty must pale and wither. Arise, therefore, and, with the whole enthusiasm of your hearts, with all the eagerness of your souls, the full fervour of your will, and the concentrated efforts of your entire being, strive to attain the paradise of His presence, and endeavour to inhale the fragrance of the incorruptible Flower, to breathe the sweet savours of holiness, and to obtain a portion of this perfume of celestial glory. Whoso followeth this counsel will break his

GOD'S COMMAND AND EXHORTATION

chains asunder, will taste the abandonment of enraptured love, will attain unto his heart's desire, and will surrender his soul into the hands of his Beloved. Bursting through his cage, he will, even as the bird of the spirit, wing his flight to his holy and everlasting nest.

Night hath succeeded day, and day hath succeeded night, and the hours and moments of your lives have come and gone, and yet none of you hath, for one instant, consented to detach himself from that which perisheth. Bestir yourselves, that the brief moments that are still yours may not be dissipated and lost. Even as the swiftness of lightning your days shall pass, and your bodies shall be laid to rest beneath a canopy of dust. What can ye then achieve? How can ye atone for your past failure?

The everlasting Candle shineth in its naked glory. Behold how it hath consumed every mortal veil. O ye moth-like lovers of His light! Brave every danger, and consecrate your souls to its consuming flame. O ye that thirst after Him! Strip yourselves of every earthly affection, and hasten to embrace your Beloved. With a zest that none can equal make haste to attain unto Him. The Flower, thus far hidden from the sight of men, is unveiled to your eyes. In the open radiance of His glory He standeth before you. His voice summoneth all the holy and sanctified beings to come and be united with Him. Happy is he that turneth thereunto; well is it with him that hath attained, and gazed on the light of so wondrous a countenance.

[*Gleanings from the Writings of Bahá'u'lláh*]

A 8. O banished and faithful friend! Quench the thirst of heedlessness with the sanctified waters of My grace, and chase the gloom of remoteness through the morning-light of My Divine presence. Suffer not the habitation wherein dwelleth My undying love for thee to be destroyed through the tyranny of covetous desires, and overcloud not the beauty of the heavenly Youth with the dust of self and passion. Clothe thyself with the essence of righteousness, and let thine heart be afraid of none except God. Obstruct not the luminous spring of thy soul with the thorns and brambles of vain and inordinate affections, and impede not the flow of the living waters that stream from the fountain of thine heart. Set all thy hope in God, and cleave tenaciously to His unfailing mercy. Who else but Him can enrich the destitute, and deliver the fallen from his abasement?

O My servants! Were ye to discover the hidden, the shoreless oceans of My incorruptible wealth, ye would, of a certainty, esteem as nothing the world, nay the entire creation. Let the flame of search burn with such fierceness within your hearts as to enable you to attain your supreme and most exalted goal—the station at which ye can draw nigh unto, and be united with, your Best-Beloved. . . .

O My servants! Let not your vain hopes and idle fancies sap the foundations of your belief in the All-Glorious God, inasmuch as such imaginings have been wholly unprofitable unto men, and failed to direct their steps unto the straight Path. Think ye, O My servants, that the Hand of My all-encompassing, My overshadowing, and transcendent sovereignty is chained up, that the flow of Mine ancient, My ceaseless, and all-pervasive mercy is checked, or that the clouds of My sublime and unsurpassed favours have ceased to rain their gifts upon men? Can ye imagine that the wondrous works that have proclaimed My divine and resistless power are withdrawn, or that the potency of My will and purpose hath been deterred from directing the destinies of mankind? If it be not so, wherefore, then, have ye striven to prevent the deathless Beauty of My sacred and gracious Countenance from being unveiled to men's eyes? Why have ye struggled to hinder the Manifestation of the Almighty and

All-Glorious Being from shedding the radiance of His Revelation upon the earth? Were ye to be fair in your judgment, ye would readily recognize how the realities of all created things are inebriated with the joy of this new and wondrous Revelation, how all the atoms of the earth have been illuminated through the brightness of its glory. Vain and wretched is that which ye have imagined and still imagine!

Retrace your steps, O My servants, and incline your hearts to Him Who is the Source of your creation. Deliver yourselves from your evil and corrupt affections, and hasten to embrace the light of the undying Fire that gloweth on the Sinai of this mysterious and transcendent Revelation. Corrupt not the holy, the all-embracing, and primal Word of God, and seek not to profane its sanctity or to debase its exalted character. O heedless ones! Though the wonders of My mercy have encompassed all created things, both visible and invisible, and though the revelations of My grace and bounty have permeated every atom of the universe, yet the rod with which I can chastise the wicked is grievous, and the fierceness of Mine anger against them terrible. With ears that are sanctified from vainglory and worldly desires hearken unto the counsels which I, in My merciful kindness, have revealed unto you, and with your inner and outer eyes contemplate the evidences of My marvellous Revelation. . . .

O My servants! Deprive not yourselves of the unfading and resplendent Light that shineth within the Lamp of Divine glory. Let the flame of the love of God burn brightly within your radiant hearts. Feed it with the oil of Divine guidance, and protect it within the shelter of your constancy. Guard it within the globe of trust and detachment from all else but God, so that the evil whisperings of the ungodly may not extinguish its light. O My servants! My holy, My divinely ordained Revelation may be likened unto an ocean in whose depths are concealed innumerable pearls of great price, of surpassing lustre. It is the duty of every seeker to bestir himself and strive to attain the shores of this ocean, so that he may, in proportion to the eagerness of his search and the efforts he hath exerted, partake of such benefits as have been pre-ordained in God's irrevocable and hidden Tablets. If no one be willing to direct his steps towards its shores, if every one should fail to arise and find Him, can such a failure be said to have robbed this ocean of its power or to have lessened, to any degree, its treasures? How vain, how contemptible, are the imaginations which your hearts have devised, and are still devising! O My servants! The one true God is My witness! This most great, this fathomless and surging Ocean is near, astonishingly near, unto you. Behold it is closer to you than your life-vein! Swift as the twinkling of an eye ye can, if ye but wish it, reach and partake of this imperishable favour, this God-given grace, this incorruptible gift, this most potent and unspeakably glorious bounty.

O My servants! Could ye apprehend with what wonders of My munificence and bounty I have willed to entrust your souls, ye would, of a truth, rid yourselves of attachment to all created things, and would gain a true knowledge of your own selves—a knowledge which is the same as the comprehension of Mine own Being. Ye would find yourselves independent of all else but Me, and would perceive, with your inner and outer eye, and as manifest as the revelation of My effulgent Name, the seas of My loving-kindness and bounty moving within you. Suffer not your idle fancies, your evil passions, your insincerity and blindness of heart to dim the lustre, or stain the sanctity, of so lofty a station. Ye are even as the bird which soareth, with the full force of its mighty wings and with complete and joyous confidence, through the immensity of the heavens, until,

GOD'S COMMAND AND EXHORTATION 65

impelled to satisfy its hunger, it turneth longingly to the water and clay of the earth below it, and, having been entrapped in the mesh of its desire, findeth itself impotent to resume its flight to the realms whence it came. Powerless to shake off the burden weighing on its sullied wings, that bird, hitherto an inmate of the heavens, is now forced to seek a dwelling-place upon the dust. Wherefore, O My servants, defile not your wings with the clay of waywardness and vain desires, and suffer them not to be stained with the dust of envy and hate, that ye may not be hindered from soaring in the heavens of My divine knowledge.

O My servants! Through the might of God and His power, and out of the treasury of His knowledge and wisdom, I have brought forth and revealed unto you the pearls that lay concealed in the depths of His everlasting ocean. I have summoned the Maids of Heaven to emerge from behind the veil of concealment, and have clothed them with these words of Mine—words of consummate power and wisdom. I have, moreover, with the hand of divine power, unsealed the choice wine of My Revelation, and have wafted its holy, its hidden, and musk-laden fragrance upon all created things. Who else but yourselves is to be blamed if ye choose to remain unendowed with so great an outpouring of God's transcendent and all-encompassing grace, with so bright a revelation of His resplendent mercy? . . .

O My servants! There shineth nothing else in Mine heart except the unfading light of the Morn of Divine guidance, and out of My mouth proceedeth naught but the essence of truth, which the Lord your God hath revealed. Follow not, therefore, your earthly desires, and violate not the Covenant of God, nor break your pledge to Him. With firm determination, with the whole affection of your heart, and with the full force of your words, turn ye unto Him, and walk not in the ways of the foolish. The world is but a show, vain and empty, a mere nothing, bearing the semblance of reality. Set not your affections upon it. Break not the bond that uniteth you with your Creator, and be not of those that have erred and strayed from His ways. Verily I say, the world is like the vapour in a desert, which the thirsty dreameth to be water and striveth after it with all his might, until when he cometh unto it, he findeth it to be mere illusion. It may, moreover, be likened unto the lifeless image of the beloved whom the lover hath sought and found, in the end, after long search and to his utmost regret, to be such as cannot " fatten nor appease his hunger ".

O My servants ! Sorrow not if, in these days and on this earthly plane, things contrary to your wishes have been ordained and manifested by God, for days of blissful joy, of heavenly delight, are assuredly in store for you. Worlds, holy and spiritually glorious, will be unveiled to your eyes. You are destined by Him, in this world and hereafter, to partake of their benefits, to share in their joys, and to obtain a portion of their sustaining grace. To each and every one of them you will, no doubt, attain.

[*Gleanings from the Writings of Bahá'u'lláh*]

A 9. Gird up the loins of thine endeavour, that haply thou mayest guide thy neighbour to the law of God, the Most Merciful. Such an act, verily, excelleth all other acts in the sight of God, the All-Possessing, the Most High. Such must be thy steadfastness in the Cause of God, that no earthly thing whatsoever will have the power to deter thee from thy duty. Though the powers of earth be leagued against thee, though all men dispute with thee, thou must remain unshaken.

Be unrestrained as the wind, while carrying the Message of

GOD'S COMMAND AND EXHORTATION

Him Who hath caused the Dawn of Divine Guidance to break. Consider, how the wind, faithful to that which God hath ordained, bloweth upon all the regions of the earth, be they inhabited or desolate. Neither the sight of desolation, nor the evidences of prosperity, can either pain or please it. It bloweth in every direction, as bidden by its Creator. So should be every one that claimeth to be a lover of the one true God. It behoveth him to fix his gaze upon the fundamentals of His Faith, and to labour diligently for its propagation. Wholly for the sake of God he should proclaim His Message, and with that same spirit accept whatever response his words may evoke in his hearer. He who shall accept and believe, shall receive his reward; and he who shall turn away, shall receive none other than his own punishment.

[*Gleanings from the Writings of Bahá'u'lláh*]

A 10. Grieve thou not over those that have busied themselves with the things of this world, and have forgotten the remembrance of God, the Most Great. By Him Who is the Eternal Truth! The day is approaching when the wrathful anger of the Almighty will have taken hold of them. He, verily, is the Omnipotent, the All-Subduing, the Most Powerful. He shall cleanse the earth from the defilement of their corruption, and shall give it for an heritage unto such of His servants as are nigh unto Him.

[*Gleanings from the Writings of Bahá'u'lláh*]

" The Hidden Words " of Bahá'u'lláh is his chief ethical work. It gives in one hundred and fifty-three sententious stanzas of poetical prose the sum and essence of the commands of all the prophets of the past. Some of these have special reference to the new Dispensation, among them the six following quotations.

B 1. O ye dwellers in the highest paradise!

Proclaim unto the children of assurance that within the realms of holiness, nigh unto the celestial paradise, a new garden hath appeared, round which circle the denizens of the realm on high and the immortal dwellers of the exalted paradise. Strive, then, that ye may attain that station, that ye may unravel the mysteries of love from its wind-flowers and learn the secret of divine and consummate wisdom from its eternal fruits. Solaced are the eyes of them that enter and abide therein!

[*The Hidden Words*, II. 18]

B 2. O dwellers of My paradise!

With the hands of loving kindness I have planted in the holy garden of paradise the young tree of your love and friendship, and have watered it with the goodly showers of My tender grace; now that the hour of its fruiting is come strive that it may be protected, and be not consumed with the flame of desire and passion.

[*The Hidden Words*, II. 34]

B 3. O children of Adam!

Holy words and pure and goodly deeds ascend unto the heaven of celestial glory. Strive that your deeds may be cleansed from the dust of self and hypocrisy and find favour at the court of glory; for ere long the assayers of mankind shall, in the holy presence of the Adored One, accept naught but absolute virtue and deeds of stainless purity. This is the day-star of wisdom and of divine mystery that hath shone above the horizon of the divine will. Blessed are they that turn thereunto.

[*The Hidden Words*, II. 69]

B 4. O son of him that stood by his own entity in the kingdom of his self!

GOD'S COMMAND AND EXHORTATION

Know thou, that I have wafted unto thee all the fragrances of holiness, have fully revealed to thee My word, have perfected through thee My bounty and have desired for thee that which I have desired for My Self. Be then content with My pleasure and thankful unto Me.

[*The Hidden Words*, I. 70]

B 5. O son of My handmaid!

Guidance hath ever been given by words, and now it is given by deeds. Everyone must show forth deeds that are pure and holy, for words are the property of all alike, whereas such deeds as these belong only to Our loved ones. Strive then with heart and soul to distinguish yourselves by your deeds. In this wise We counsel you in this holy and resplendent tablet.

[*The Hidden Words*, II. 76]

Envoi

B 6. The mystic and wondrous Bride, hidden ere this beneath the veiling of utterance, hath now, by the grace of God and His divine favour, been made manifest even as the resplendent light shed by the beauty of the Beloved. I bear witness, O friends! that the favour is complete, the argument fulfilled, the proof manifest and the evidence established. Let it now be seen what your endeavours in the path of detachment will reveal. In this wise hath the divine favour been fully vouchsafed unto you and unto them that are in heaven and on earth. All praise to God, the Lord of all Worlds.

[*The Hidden Words*, II. Epilogue]

CHAPTER III

THE PROCLAMATION OF THE DAY OF GOD

The Address attributed to the Báb before he sent out his Apostles on their Mission.

The Báb claimed to be the promised " Qá'im " and also the Herald of a Prophet immeasurably greater than himself. He made his Declaration to his first believer, Mullá Ḥusayn, on May 22, 1844, and within a period of a few weeks other seekers for the expected Prophet were by degrees led to discover the object of their quest and to enter the Báb's presence. Having given them special instructions he bade them scatter far and wide through the provinces of their native land where they inaugurated " a tumult that convulsed their country and sent its echoes reverberating as far as the capitals of western Europe ".

A 1. O My beloved friends ! You are the bearers of the name of God in this Day. You have been chosen as the repositories of His mystery. It behoves each one of you to manifest the attributes of God, and to exemplify by your deeds and words the signs of His righteousness, His power and glory. The very members of your body must bear witness to the loftiness of your purpose, the integrity of your life, the reality of your faith, and the exalted character of your devotion. For verily I say, this is the Day spoken of by God in His Book : " On that day will We set a seal upon their mouths ; yet shall their hands speak unto Us, and their feet shall bear witness to that which they shall have done." Ponder the words of Jesus addressed to His disciples, as He sent them forth to propagate the Cause of God. In words such as these, He bade them arise and fulfil their mission: "Ye are even as the fire which in the darkness of the night has been kindled upon the mountain-top. Let your light shine before the eyes of men. Such must be the purity of your character and the degree of your renunciation, that the people of the earth may through you recognize and be drawn closer to the heavenly Father who is the Source of purity and grace. For none has seen the Father who is in heaven. You who are His spiritual children must by your deeds exemplify His virtues, and witness to His glory. You are the salt of the earth, but if the salt have lost its savour, wherewith shall it be salted? Such must be the degree of your detachment, that into whatever city you enter to proclaim and teach the Cause of God, you should in no wise expect either meat or reward from its people. Nay, when you depart out of that city, you should shake the dust from off your feet. As you have entered it pure and undefiled, so must you depart from that city. For verily I say, the heavenly Father is ever with you and keeps watch over you. If you be faithful to Him, He will assuredly deliver into your hands all the treasures of the earth, and will exalt you above all the rulers and kings of the world." O My Letters! Verily I say, immensely exalted is this Day above the days of the Apostles of old. Nay, immeasurable is the difference! You are the witnesses of the Dawn of the promised Day of God. You are the partakers of the mystic chalice of His Revelation. Gird up the loins of endeavour, and be mindful of the words of God as revealed in His Book[1]: "Lo, the Lord thy God is come, and with Him is the company of His angels arrayed before Him." Purge your hearts of worldly desires, and let angelic virtues be your adorning. Strive that by your deeds you may bear witness to the truth of these words of God, and beware lest, by " turning back ", He may " change you for another people ", who " shall not be your

[1] The Qur'án.

like ", and who shall take from you the Kingdom of God. The days when idle worship was deemed sufficient are ended. The time is come when naught but the purest motive, supported by deeds of stainless purity, can ascend to the throne of the Most High and be acceptable unto Him. " The good word riseth up unto Him, and the righteous deed will cause it to be exalted before Him." You are the lowly, of whom God has thus spoken in His Book [1] : " And We desire to show favour to those who were brought low in the land, and to make them Our heirs." You have been called to this station ; you will attain to it, only if you arise to trample beneath your feet every earthly desire, and endeavour to become those " honoured servants of His who speak not till He hath spoken, and who do His bidding ". You are the first Letters that have been generated from the Primal Point,[2] the first Springs that have welled out from the Source of this Revelation. Beseech the Lord your God to grant that no earthly entanglements, no worldly affections, no ephemeral pursuits, may tarnish the purity, or embitter the sweetness, of that grace which flows through you. I am preparing you for the advent of a mighty Day. Exert your utmost endeavour that, in the world to come, I, who am now instructing you, may, before the mercy-seat of God, rejoice in your deeds and glory in your achievements. The secret of the Day that is to come is now concealed. It can neither be divulged nor estimated. The newly-born babe of that Day excels the wisest and most venerable men of this time, and the lowliest and most unlearned of that period shall surpass in understanding the most erudite and accomplished divines of this age. Scatter throughout the length and breadth of this land, and, with steadfast feet and sanctified hearts, prepare the way for His coming. Heed not your weaknesses and frailty ; fix your gaze upon the invincible

[1] The Qur'án. [2] One of the titles of the Báb.

power of the Lord, your God, the Almighty. Has He not, in past days, caused Abraham, in spite of His seeming helplessness, to triumph over the forces of Nimrod? Has He not enabled Moses, whose staff was His only companion, to vanquish Pharaoh and his hosts? Has He not established the ascendancy of Jesus, poor and lowly as He was in the eyes of men, over the combined forces of the Jewish people? Has He not subjected the barbarous and militant tribes of Arabia to the holy and transforming discipline of Muḥammad, His Prophet? Arise in His name, put your trust wholly in Him, and be assured of ultimate victory.

[*The Dawn-Breakers*, pp. 92-4]

Bahá'u'lláh proclaims to mankind the Opening of a New Revelation and the Advent of the Day of God promised from the foundation of the World.

B 1. The Revelation which, from time immemorial, hath been acclaimed as the Purpose and Promise of all the Prophets of God, and the most cherished Desire of His Messengers, hath now, by virtue of the pervasive Will of the Almighty and at His irresistible bidding, been revealed unto men. The advent of such a Revelation hath been heralded in all the sacred Scriptures. Behold how, notwithstanding such an announcement, mankind hath strayed from its path and shut out itself from its glory.

Say: O ye lovers of the One true God! Strive, that ye may truly recognize and know Him, and observe befittingly His precepts. This is a Revelation, under which, if a man shed for its sake one drop of blood, myriads of oceans will be his recompense. Take heed, O friends, that ye forfeit not so inestimable a benefit, or disregard its transcendent station . . .

[*Gleanings from the Writings of Bahá'u'lláh*]

B 2. This is the Day in which God's most excellent favours have been poured out upon men, the Day in which His most mighty grace hath been infused into all created things. It is incumbent upon all the peoples of the world to reconcile their differences, and, with perfect unity and peace, abide beneath the shadow of the Tree of His care and loving-kindness. It behoveth them to cleave to whatsoever will, in this Day, be conducive to the exaltation of their stations, and to the promotion of their best interests. Happy are those whom the all-glorious Pen was moved to remember, and blessed are those men whose names, by virtue of Our inscrutable decree, We have preferred to conceal.

Beseech ye the one true God to grant that all men may be graciously assisted to fulfil that which is acceptable in Our sight. Soon will the present-day order be rolled up, and a new one spread out in its stead. Verily, thy Lord speaketh the truth, and is the Knower of things unseen.

[*Gleanings from the Writings of Bahá'u'lláh*]

B 3. This is the Day whereon the Ocean of God's mercy hath been manifested unto men, the Day in which the Day Star of His loving-kindness hath shed its radiance upon them, the Day in which the clouds of His bountiful favour have overshadowed the whole of mankind. Now is the time to cheer and refresh the down-cast through the invigorating breeze of love and fellowship, and the living waters of friendliness and charity.

They who are the beloved of God, in whatever place they gather and whomsoever they may meet, must evince, in their attitude toward God, and in the manner of their celebration of His praise and glory, such humility and submissiveness that every atom of the dust beneath their feet may attest the depth of their devotion. The conversation carried by these holy souls should be informed with such power that these same atoms of dust will be thrilled by its influence. They should conduct themselves in such manner that the earth upon which they tread may never be allowed to address to them such words as these : " I am to be preferred above you. For witness, how patient I am in bearing the burden which the husbandman layeth upon me. I am the instrument that continually imparteth unto all beings the blessings with which He Who is the Source of all grace hath entrusted me. Notwithstanding the honour conferred upon me, and the unnumbered evidences of my wealth—a wealth that supplieth the needs of all creation—behold the measure of my humility, witness with what absolute submissiveness I allow myself to be trodden beneath the feet of men. . . ."

Show forbearance and benevolence and love to one another. Should any one among you be incapable of grasping a certain truth, or be striving to comprehend it, show forth, when conversing with him, a spirit of extreme kindliness and good-will. Help him to see and recognize the truth, without esteeming yourself to be, in the least, superior to him, or to be possessed of greater endowments.

The whole duty of man in this Day is to attain that share of the flood of grace which God poureth forth for him. Let none, therefore, consider the largeness or smallness of the receptacle. The portion of some might lie in the palm of a man's hand, the portion of others might fill a cup, and of others even a gallon-measure.

Every eye, in this Day, should seek what will best promote the Cause of God. He, Who is the Eternal Truth, beareth Me witness ! Nothing whatever can, in this Day, inflict a greater harm upon this Cause than dissension and strife, contention, estrangement and apathy, among the loved ones of God. Flee them, through the power of God and His sovereign aid, and strive ye to knit together the hearts of men, in His Name, the Unifier, the All-Knowing, the All-Wise.

Beseech ye the one true God to grant that ye may taste the savour of such deeds as are performed in His path, and partake of the sweetness of such humility and submissiveness as are shown for His sake. Forget your own selves, and turn your eyes toward your neighbour. Bend your energies to whatever may foster the education of men. Nothing is, or can ever be, hidden from God. If ye follow in His way, His incalculable and imperishable blessings will be showered upon you. This is the luminous Tablet, whose verses have streamed from the moving Pen of Him Who is the Lord of all worlds. Ponder it in your hearts, and be ye of them that observe its precepts.

[*Gleanings from the Writings of Bahá'u'lláh*]

B 4. Verily I say, this is the Day in which mankind can behold the Face, and hear the Voice, of the Promised One. The Call of God hath been raised, and the light of His countenance hath been lifted up upon men. It behoveth every man to blot out the trace of every idle word from the tablet of his heart, and to gaze, with an open and unbiased mind, on the signs of His Revelation, the proofs of His Mission, and the tokens of His glory.

Great indeed is this Day ! The allusions made to it in all the sacred Scriptures as the Day of God attest its greatness. The soul of every Prophet of God, of every Divine Messenger, hath thirsted for this wondrous Day. All the divers kindreds of the earth have, likewise, yearned to attain it. No sooner, however, had the Day Star of His Revelation manifested itself in the heaven of God's Will, than all, except those whom the Almighty was pleased to guide, were found dumbfounded and heedless.

O thou that hast remembered Me ! The most grievous veil

hath shut out the peoples of the earth from His glory, and hindered them from hearkening to His call. God grant that the light of unity may envelop the whole earth, and that the seal, " the Kingdom is God's ", may be stamped upon the brow of all its peoples.

[*Gleanings from the Writings of Bahá'u'lláh*]

B 5. The time fore-ordained unto the peoples and kindreds of the earth is now come. The promises of God, as recorded in the holy Scriptures, have all been fulfilled. Out of Zion hath gone forth the Law of God, and Jerusalem, and the hills and land thereof, are filled with the glory of His Revelation. Happy is the man that pondereth in his heart that which hath been revealed in the Books of God, the Help in Peril, the Self-Subsisting. Meditate upon this, O ye beloved of God, and let your ears be attentive unto His Word, so that ye may, by His grace and mercy, drink your fill from the crystal waters of constancy, and become as steadfast and immovable as the mountain in His Cause.

In the Book of Isaiah it is written : " Enter into the rock, and hide thee in the dust, for fear of the Lord, and for the glory of His majesty." No man that meditateth upon this verse can fail to recognize the greatness of this Cause, or doubt the exalted character of this Day—the Day of God Himself. This same verse is followed by these words : " And the Lord alone shall be exalted in that Day." This is the Day which the Pen of the Most High hath glorified in all the holy Scriptures. There is no verse in them that doth not declare the glory of His holy Name, and no Book that doth not testify unto the loftiness of this most exalted theme. Were We to make mention of all that hath been revealed in these heavenly Books and holy Scriptures concerning this Revelation, this Tablet would assume impossible dimensions. It is incumbent, in this Day, upon every man to place his whole trust in the manifold bounties of God, and arise to disseminate, with the utmost wisdom, the verities of His Cause. Then, and only then, will the whole earth be enveloped with the morning light of His Revelation.

[*Gleanings from the Writings of Bahá'u'lláh*]

'Abdu'l-Bahá delivers the Message direct to the western world and carries it in person to many parts of Europe and America.

C 1. Do you know in what Day you are living ? Do you realize in what Dispensation you are alive ? Have you not read in the Holy Scriptures that at the consummation of the ages there shall appear a Day which is the Sun of all the past Days ? This is the Day in which the Lord of Hosts has come down from heaven on the clouds of glory ! This is the Day in which the inhabitants of all the world shall enter under the shelter of the Word of God.

This is the Day whose real sovereign is His Highness the Almighty. This is the Day when the East and the West shall embrace each other like unto two lovers. This is the Day in which war and contention shall be forgotten. This is the Day in which nations and governments will enter into an eternal bond of amity and conciliation. This Century is the fulfilment of the Promised Century.

This Day is the dawn of the appearances of the traces of the glorious visions of the past prophets and sages.

Now is the dawn ; ere long the effulgent Sun shall rise and station itself in the meridian of its majesty. Then you shall observe the effects of the Sun. Then you shall behold what heavenly illumination has become manifest. Then you shall comprehend that these are the infinite bestowals of God ! Then you shall see that this world has become another world. Then you shall perceive that the Teachings of God have universally spread.

Rest ye assured that this darkness shall be dispelled and these impenetrable clouds which have darkened the horizon shall be scattered, and the Sun of Reality shall appear in its full splendour. Its rays shall melt the icebergs of hatred and differences which have transformed the moving sea of humanity into hard frozen immensity. The vices of the world of nature shall be changed into praiseworthy attributes, and the lights of the excellences of the Divine realm shall appear.

The principles of Bahá'u'lláh, like unto the spirit, shall penetrate the dead body of the world, and the Love of God, like unto an artery, shall beat through the heart of the five continents.

The East shall become illumined, the West perfumed, and the children of men shall enter beneath the all-embracing canopy of the oneness of the world of humanity.

In this Day the rest of the people are asleep. Praise be to God that you are awakened! They are all uninformed, but praise be to God you are informed of the mysteries of God! Thank ye God that in this arena you have preceded others. I hope that each one of you may become a pillar of the palace of the oneness of the world of humanity. May each one of you become a luminous star of this heaven, thus lighting the path of those who are seeking the goal of human perfection.

[*Star of the West*, IV. 6]

C 2. O ye beloved of God! O ye children of His Kingdom!

Verily, verily the new heaven and the new earth are come. The holy City, new Jerusalem, hath come down from on high in the form of a maid of heaven, veiled, beauteous, and unique, and prepared for reunion with her lovers on earth. The angelic company of the celestial Concourse have joined in a call that hath rung throughout the universe, all loudly and mightily acclaiming : " Hail, O City of God ! Abide Thou, and make Thy habitation with the pure, virtuous and holy servants of Thine ; for they are Thy people, and Thou art their Lord."

He hath wiped away their tears, kindled their light, rejoiced their hearts and enraptured their souls. Death shall no more overtake them, neither shall sorrow, crying and tribulation afflict them. The Lord God Omnipotent hath been enthroned in his Kingdom and hath made all things new. This is the truth, and what truth greater than the Revelation of St. John the divine ? He is the Alpha and Omega. He is the One that will give unto him that is athirst of the fountain of the water of life, and bestow upon the sick the remedy of true salvation. He whom such grace aideth is verily he that receiveth the most glorious heritage from the prophets of God and His holy ones. The Lord will be his God, and he His dearly-beloved Son.

Rejoice, then, O ye beloved of the Lord and His chosen ones, and ye the children of God and His people, raise your voice and laud and magnify the Lord, the Most High ; for His light hath beamed forth, His signs have appeared, and the billows of His rising ocean have scattered on every shore many a precious pearl.

[*Star of the West*, XIV. 12]

CHAPTER IV

THE JOURNEY OF THE SOUL

A. GOD AND THE UNIVERSE

1. *One God*

God Testifieth to the Unity of His Godhood and to the singleness of His own Being. On the throne of eternity, from the inaccessible heights of His station, His tongue proclaimeth that there is none other God but Him. He Himself, independently of all else, hath ever been a witness unto His own oneness, the revealer of His own nature, the glorifier of His own essence. He, verily, is the All-Powerful, the Almighty, the Beauteous.

He is supreme over His servants, and standeth over His creatures. In His hand is the source of authority and truth. He maketh men alive by His signs, and causeth them to die through His wrath. He shall not be asked of His doings and His might is equal unto all things. He is the Potent, the All-Subduing. He holdeth within His grasp the empire of all things, and on His right hand is fixed the Kingdom of His Revelation. His power, verily, embraceth the whole of creation. Victory and over-lordship are His; all might and dominion are His; all glory and greatness are His. He, of a truth, is the All-Glorious, the Most Powerful, the Unconditioned.

[*Prayers and Meditations of Bahá'u'lláh*]

" *Some Answered Questions* ", *from which are taken the passages in this section numbered A 2, 3 ; B 5, 6 ; D 5, is a book of 'Abdu'l-Bahá's table-talk in 'Akká while he was still a prisoner. It is the chief repository of his teachings on Christian subjects and on what he would speak of as " divine science ".*

2. One Law

Nature is that condition, that reality, which in appearance consists in life and death, or in other words, in the composition and decomposition of all things.

This Nature is subjected to an absolute organization, to determined laws, to a complete order and a finished design, from which it will never depart ; to such a degree, indeed, that if you look carefully and with keen sight, from the smallest invisible atom up to such large bodies of the world of existence as the globe of the sun or other great stars and luminous spheres, whether you regard their arrangement, their composition, their form or their movement, you will find that all are in the highest degree of organization, and are under one law from which they will never depart.

[*Some Answered Questions*]

3. *The Succession of Cycles*

Each one of the luminous bodies in this limitless firmament has a cycle of revolution which is of a different duration, and every one revolves in its own orbit, and again begins a new cycle. So the earth, every three hundred and sixty-five days, five hours, forty-eight minutes and a fraction, completes a revolution ; and then it begins a new cycle, that is to say, the first cycle is again renewed. In the same way, for the whole universe, whether for the heavens or for men, there are cycles of great events, of important facts and occurrences. When a cycle is ended, a new cycle begins, and the old one, on account of the great events which take place, is completely forgotten, and not a trace or record of it will remain. As you see, we have no records of twenty thousand years ago, although we have before proved by argument that life on this earth is very ancient. It is not one hundred thousand, or two hundred thousand, or one million or two million years old ; it is very ancient, and the ancient records and traces are entirely obliterated.

Each of the Divine Manifestations has likewise a cycle, and during the cycle His laws and commandments prevail and are performed. When His cycle is completed by the appearance of a new Manifestation, a new cycle begins. In this way cycles begin, end, and are renewed, until a universal cycle is completed in the world, when important events and great occurrences will take place which entirely efface every trace and every record of the past ; then a new universal cycle begins in the world, for this universe has no beginning. We have before stated proofs and evidences concerning this subject ; there is no need of repetition.

Briefly, we say a universal cycle in the world of existence signifies a long duration of time, and innumerable and incalculable periods and epochs. In such a cycle the Manifestations appear with splendour in the realm of the visible, until a great and universal Manifestation makes the world the centre of His radiance. His appearance causes the world to attain to maturity, and the extension of His cycle is very great. Afterwards other Manifestations will arise under His shadow, who according to the needs of the time will renew certain commandments relating to material questions and affairs, while remaining under His shadow.

We are in the cycle which began with Adam, and its universal Manifestation is Bahá'u'lláh.

[*Some Answered Questions*]

B. THE PROCEEDING OF MAN FROM GOD

1. O Son of Man!

Veiled in My immemorial being and in the ancient eternity of My essence, I knew My love for thee; therefore I created thee, have engraved on thee Mine image and revealed to thee My beauty.

[*The Hidden Words*, I. 3]

2. O Son of Bounty!

Out of the wastes of nothingness, with the clay of My command I made thee to appear, and have ordained for thy training every atom in existence and the essence of all created things. Thus, ere thou didst issue from thy mother's womb, I destined for thee two founts of gleaming milk, eyes to watch over thee, and hearts to love thee. Out of My loving-kindness, neath the shade of My mercy I nurtured thee, and guarded thee by the essence of My grace and favour. And My purpose in all this was that thou mightest attain My everlasting dominion and become worthy of My invisible bestowals.

[*The Hidden Words*, II. 29]

3. And now, concerning thy question regarding the creation of man. Know thou that all men have been created in the nature made by God, the Guardian, the Self-Subsisting. Unto each one hath been prescribed a pre-ordained measure, as decreed in God's mighty and guarded Tablets. All that which ye potentially possess can, however, be manifested only as a result of your own volition.

[*Gleanings from the Writings of Bahá'u'lláh*]

4. Thou hast asked Me concerning the nature of the soul. Know, verily, that the soul is a sign of God, a heavenly gem whose reality the most learned of men hath failed to grasp, and

whose mystery no mind, however acute, can ever hope to unravel. It is the first among all created things to declare the excellence of its Creator, the first to recognize His glory, to cleave to His truth, and to bow down in adoration before Him. If it be faithful to God, it will reflect His light, and will, eventually, return unto Him. If it fail, however, in its allegiance to its Creator, it will become a victim to self and passion, and will, in the end, sink in their depths.

[*Gleanings from the Writings of Bahá'u'lláh*]

5. The beginning of the existence of man on the terrestrial globe resembles his formation in the womb of the mother. The embryo in the womb of the mother gradually grows and develops until birth, after which it continues to grow and develop until it reaches the age of discretion and maturity. Though in infancy the signs of the mind and spirit appear in man, they do not reach the degree of perfection ; they are imperfect. Only when man attains maturity do the mind and the spirit appear and become evident in utmost perfection.

So also the formation of man in the matrix of the world was in the beginning like the embryo ; then gradually he made progress in perfection, and grew and developed until he reached the state of maturity, when the mind and spirit became visible in the greatest power. In the beginning of his formation the mind and spirit also existed, but they were hidden ; later they were manifested. In the womb of the world mind and spirit also existed in the embryo, but they were concealed ; afterwards they appeared. So it is that in the seed the tree exists, but it is hidden and concealed ; when it develops and grows, the complete tree appears. In the same way the growth and development of all beings is gradual ; this is the universal divine organization, and the natural system. The seed does not at once become a tree, the embryo does not at once become a man, the mineral does not suddenly become a stone. No, they grow and develop gradually, and attain the limit of perfection.

All beings, whether large or small, were created perfect and complete from the first, but their perfections appear in them by degrees. The organization of God is one: the evolution of existence is one: the divine system is one. Whether they be small or great beings, all are subject to one law and system. Each seed has in it from the first all the vegetable perfections. For example, in the seed all the vegetable perfections exist from the beginning, but not visibly; afterwards little by little they appear. So it is first the shoot which appears from the seed, then the branches, leaves, blossoms, and fruits; but from the beginning of its existence all these things are in the seed, potentially, though not apparently.

In the same way, the embryo possesses from the first all perfections, such as the spirit, the mind, the sight, the smell, the taste—in one word, all the powers—but they are not visible, and become so only by degrees.

Similarly, the terrestrial globe from the beginning was created with all its elements, substances, minerals, atoms, and organisms; but these only appeared by degrees: first the mineral, then the plant, afterward the animal, and finally man. But from the first these kinds and species existed, but were undeveloped in the terrestrial globe, and then appeared only gradually. For the supreme organization of God, and the universal natural system, surrounds all beings, and all are subject to this rule. When you consider this universal system, you see that there is not one of the beings, which at its coming into existence has reached the limit of perfection. No, they gradually grow and develop, and then attain the degree of perfection.

[*Some Answered Questions*]

6. The wisdom of the appearance of the spirit in the body is this : the human spirit is a divine trust, and it must traverse all conditions, for its passage and movement through the conditions of existence will be the means of its acquiring perfections . . . Even in the condition of the body it will surely acquire perfections.

Besides this, it is necessary that the signs of the perfection of the spirit should be apparent in this world, so that the world of creation may bring forth endless results, and this body may receive life and manifest the divine bounties . . . If there were no man, the perfections of the spirit would not appear, and the light of the mind would not be resplendent in this world. The world would be like a body without a soul. . . .

The reflection of the divine perfections appears in the reality of man so he is the representative of God, the messenger of God. If man did not exist, the universe would be without result, for the object of existence is the appearance of the perfections of God.

[*Some Answered Questions*]

C. THE RETURN OF MAN TO GOD

1. O Son of Being !

Thy Paradise is My love ; thy heavenly home, reunion with Me. Enter therein and tarry not. This is that which hath been destined for thee in Our Kingdom above and Our exalted Dominion.

[*The Hidden Words*, I. 6]

O Son of Spirit !

There is no peace for thee save by renouncing thyself and turning unto Me ; for it behoveth thee to glory in My name not in thine own; to put thy trust in Me and not in thyself, since I desire to be loved alone and above all that is.

[*The Hidden Words*, I. 8]

O Son of Being!

My love is My stronghold; he that entereth therein is safe and secure, and he that turneth away shall surely stray and perish.

[*The Hidden Words*, I. 9]

O Son of Spirit!

The spirit of holiness beareth unto thee the joyful tidings of reunion; wherefore dost thou grieve? The spirit of power confirmeth thee in His cause; why dost thou veil thyself? The light of His countenance doth lead thee; how canst thou go astray?

[*The Hidden Words*, I. 34]

O Son of Man!

Sorrow not save that thou art far from Us. Rejoice not save that thou art drawing near and returning unto Us.

[*The Hidden Words*, I. 35]

O Son of Man!

Rejoice in the gladness of thine heart, that thou mayest be worthy to meet Me and to mirror forth My beauty.

[*The Hidden Words*, I, 36]

2. O my brother, when a true seeker determines to take the step of search in the path leading to the knowledge of the Ancient of Days, he must, before all else, cleanse and purify his heart, which is the seat of the revelation of the inner mysteries of God, from the obscuring dust of all acquired knowledge, and the allusions of the embodiments of satanic fancy. He must

purge his breast, which is the sanctuary of the abiding love of the Beloved, of every defilement, and sanctify his soul from all that pertaineth to water and clay, from all shadowy and ephemeral attachments. He must so cleanse his heart that no remnant of either love or hate may linger therein, lest that love blindly incline him to error, or that hate repel him away from the truth. Even as thou dost witness in this day how most of the people, because of such love and hate, are bereft of the immortal Face, have strayed far from the Embodiments of the divine mysteries, and, shepherdless, are roaming through the wilderness of oblivion and error. That seeker must at all times put his trust in God, must renounce the peoples of the earth, detach himself from the world of dust, and cleave unto Him Who is the Lord of Lords. He must never seek to exalt himself above any one, must wash away from the tablet of his heart every trace of pride and vain-glory, must cling unto patience and resignation, observe silence, and refrain from idle talk. For the tongue is a smouldering fire, and excess of speech a deadly poison. Material fire consumeth the body, whereas the fire of the tongue devoureth both heart and soul. The force of the former lasteth but for a time, whilst the effects of the latter endure a century.

That seeker should also regard backbiting as grievous error, and keep himself aloof from its dominion, inasmuch as backbiting quencheth the light of the heart, and extinguisheth the life of the soul. He should be content with little, and be freed from all inordinate desire. He should treasure the companionship of those that have renounced the world, and regard avoidance of boastful and worldly people a precious benefit. At the dawn of every day he should commune with God, and with all his soul persevere in the quest of his Beloved. He should consume every wayward thought with the flame of His loving mention, and, with the swiftness of lightning, pass by all else save Him. He should succour the dispossessed, and never withhold his favour from the destitute. He should show kindness to animals, how much more unto his fellow-man, to him who is endowed with the power of utterance. He should not hesitate to offer up his life for his Beloved, nor allow the censure of the people to turn him away from the Truth. He should not wish for others that which he doth not wish for himself, nor promise that which he doth not fulfil. With all his heart should the seeker avoid fellowship with evil doers, and pray for the remission of their sins. He should forgive the sinful, and never despise his low estate, for none knoweth what his own end shall be. How often hath a sinner, at the hour of death, attained to the essence of faith, and, quaffing the immortal draught, hath taken his flight unto the celestial Concourse. And how often hath a devout believer, at the hour of his soul's ascension, been so changed as to fall into the nethermost fire. Our purpose in revealing these convincing and weighty utterances is to impress upon the seeker that he should regard all else beside God as transient, and count all things save Him, Who is the Object of all adoration, as utter nothingness.

These are among the attributes of the exalted, and constitute the hall-mark of the spiritually-minded. They have already been mentioned in connection with the requirements of the wayfarers that tread the Path of Positive Knowledge. When the detached wayfarer and sincere seeker hath fulfilled these essential conditions, then and only then can he be called a true seeker. Whensoever he hath fulfilled the conditions implied in the verse: "Whoso maketh efforts for Us," he shall enjoy the blessing conferred by the words: "In Our ways shall We assuredly guide him."

Only when the lamp of search, of earnest striving, of longing desire, of passionate devotion, of fervid love, of rapture, and ecstasy, is kindled within the seeker's heart, and the breeze of His loving-kindness is wafted upon his soul, will the darkness of error be dispelled, the mists of doubts and misgivings be dissipated, and the lights of knowledge and certitude envelop his being. At that hour will the mystic Herald, bearing the joyful tidings of the Spirit, shine forth from the City of God resplendent as the morn, and, through the trumpet-blast of knowledge, will awaken the heart, the soul, and the spirit from the slumber of negligence. Then will the manifold favours and outpouring grace of the holy and everlasting Spirit confer such new life upon the seeker that he will find himself endowed with a new eye, a new ear, a new heart, and a new mind. He will contemplate the manifest signs of the universe, and will penetrate the hidden mysteries of the soul. Gazing with the eye of God, he will perceive within every atom a door that leadeth him to the stations of absolute certitude. He will discover in all things the mysteries of divine Revelation and the evidences of an everlasting manifestation.

I swear by God! Were he that treadeth the path of guidance and seeketh to scale the heights of righteousness to attain unto this glorious and supreme station, he would inhale at a distance of a thousand leagues the fragrance of God, and would perceive the resplendent morn of a divine Guidance rising above the dayspring of all things. Each and every thing, however small, would be to him a revelation, leading him to his Beloved, the Object of his quest. So great shall be the discernment of this seeker that he will discriminate between truth and falsehood even as he doth distinguish the sun from shadow. If in the uttermost corners of the East the sweet savours of God be wafted, he will assuredly recognize and inhale their fragrance, even though he be dwelling in the uttermost ends of the West. He will likewise clearly distinguish all the signs of God—His wondrous utterances,

His great works, and mighty deeds—from the doings, words and ways of men, even as the jeweller who knoweth the gem from the stone, or the man who distinguisheth the spring from autumn and heat from cold. When the channel of the human soul is cleansed of all worldly and impeding attachments, it will unfailingly perceive the breath of the Beloved across immeasurable distances, and will, led by its perfume, attain and enter the City of Certitude. Therein he will discern the wonders of His ancient wisdom, and will perceive all the hidden teachings from the rustling leaves of the Tree—which flourisheth in that City. With both his inner and his outer ear he will hear from its dust the hymns of glory and praise ascending unto the Lord of Lords, and with his inner eye will he discover the mysteries of " return " and " revival ". How unspeakably glorious are the signs, the tokens, the revelations, and splendours which He who is the King of names and attributes hath destined for that City ! The attainment of this City quencheth thirst without water, and kindleth the love of God without fire. Within every blade of grass are enshrined the mysteries of an inscrutable wisdom, and upon every rosebush a myriad nightingales pour out, in blissful rapture, their melody. Its wondrous tulips unfold the mystery of the Burning Bush, and its sweet savours of holiness breathe the perfume of the Messianic Spirit. It bestoweth wealth without gold, and conferreth immortality without death. In every leaf ineffable delights are treasured, and within every chamber unnumbered mysteries lie hidden.

They that valiantly labour in quest of God, will, when once they have renounced all else but Him, be so attached and wedded unto that City, that a moment's separation from it would to them be unthinkable. They will hearken unto infallible proofs from the Hyacinth of that assembly, and will receive the surest testimonies from the beauty of its Rose, and the melody of its

THE JOURNEY OF THE SOUL

Nightingale. Once in about a thousand years shall this City be renewed and readorned....

That City is none other than the Word of God revealed in every age and dispensation. In the days of Moses it was the Pentateuch; in the days of Jesus, the Gospel; in the days of Muḥammad, the Messenger of God, the Qur'án; in this day, the Bayán; and in the Dispensation of Him Whom God will make manifest, His own Book—the Book unto which all the Books of former Dispensations must needs be referred, the Book that standeth amongst them all transcendent and supreme.

[*The Book of Certitude*]

3. Since I noted thy mention of thy death in God, and thy life through Him, and thy love for the beloved of God, and the Manifestations of His Names and Dawning-Points of His Attributes—I therefore reveal unto thee sacred and resplendent tokens from the planes of glory, to attract thee unto the court of holiness and nearness and beauty, and draw thee to a station wherein thou shalt see nothing in creation save the Face of thy Beloved One, the Honoured, and behold all created things only as in the day wherein none hath a mention.

Peace be upon him who followeth the Right Path!

The stages that mark the wayfarer's journey from the abode of dust to the heavenly homeland are said to be seven. Some have called these Seven Valleys, and others, Seven Cities. And they say that until the wayfarer taketh leave of self, and traverseth these stages, he shall never reach to the ocean of nearness and union, nor drink of the peerless wine. The first is THE VALLEY OF SEARCH. The steed of this Valley is patience; without patience the wayfarer on this journey will reach nowhere and attain no goal. Nor should he ever be downhearted; if he strive for a hundred thousand years and yet fail to behold the beauty of the Friend, he should not falter. For those who seek the Ka'bih of " for Us " rejoice in the tidings: " In Our ways will We guide them." In their search, they have stoutly girded up the loins of service, and seek at every moment to journey from the plane of heedlessness into the realm of being. No bond shall hold them back, and no counsel shall deter them.

The true seeker hunteth naught but the object of his quest, and the lover hath no desire save union with his beloved. Nor shall the seeker reach his goal unless he sacrifice all things. That is, whatever he hath seen, and heard, and understood, all must be set at naught, that he may enter the realm of the spirit, which is the City of God. Labour is needed, if we are to seek Him; ardour is needed, if we are to drink of the honey of reunion with Him; and if we taste of this cup, we shall cast away the world.

On this journey the traveller abideth in every land and dwelleth in every region. In every face, he seeketh the beauty of the Friend; in every country he looketh for the Beloved. He joineth every company, and seeketh fellowship with every soul, that haply in some mind he may uncover the secret of the Friend, or in some face he may behold the beauty of the Loved One.

And if, by the help of God, he findeth on this journey a trace of the traceless Friend, and inhaleth the fragrance of the long-lost Joseph from the heavenly messenger, he shall straightway step into THE VALLEY OF LOVE and be dissolved in the fire of love.

The steed of this Valley is pain; and if there be no pain this journey will never end. In this station the lover hath no thought save the Beloved, and seeketh no refuge save the Friend. At every moment he offereth a hundred lives in the path of the Loved One, at every step he throweth a thousand heads at the feet of the Beloved.

Wherefore, O friend, give up thy self that thou mayest find the Peerless One, pass by this mortal earth that thou mayest seek a home in the nest of heaven. Be as naught, if thou wouldst kindle the fire of being and be fit for the pathway of love.

> Love seizeth not upon a living soul,
> The falcon preyeth not on a dead mouse.

Wherefore must the veils of the satanic self be burned away at the fire of love, that the spirit may be purified and cleansed and thus may know the station of the Lord of the Worlds.

> Kindle the fire of love and burn away all things,
> Then set thy foot into the land of the lovers.

And if, confirmed by the Creator, the lover escapes from the claws of the eagle of love, he will enter THE VALLEY OF KNOWLEDGE and come out of doubt into certitude, and turn from the darkness of illusion to the guiding light of the fear of God. His inner eyes will open and he will privily converse with his Beloved; he will set wide the gate of truth and piety, and shut the doors of vain imaginings. He in this station is content with the decree of God, and seeth war as peace, and findeth in death the secrets of everlasting life.

There was once a lover who had sighed for long years in separation from his beloved, and wasted in the fire of remoteness. From the rule of love, his heart was empty of patience, and his body weary of his spirit; he reckoned life without her as a mockery, and time consumed him away. How many a day he found no rest in longing for her; how many a night the pain of her kept him from sleep; his body was worn to a sigh, his heart's wound had turned him to a cry of sorrow. He had given a thousand lives for one taste of the cup of her presence, but it availed him not. The doctors knew no cure for him, and companions avoided his company; yea, physicians have no medicine for one sick of love, unless the favour of the beloved one deliver him.

At last, the tree of his longing yielded the fruit of despair, and the fire of his hope fell to ashes. Then one night he could live no more, and he went out of his house and made for the market-place. On a sudden, a watchman followed after him. He broke into a run, with the watchman following; then other watchmen came together, and barred every passage to the weary one. And the wretched one cried from his heart, and ran here and there, and moaned to himself: " Surely this watchman is the angel of death, following so fast upon me; or he is a tyrant of men, seeking to harm me." Wherefore that victim of love continued running and lamenting until he reached a garden wall, and with untold pain scaled it, for it proved very high. Then disregarding his safety, he threw himself into the garden below.

And there he beheld his beloved with a lamp in her hand, searching for a ring she had lost. When the heart-surrendered lover looked on his ravishing love, he drew a great breath and raised up his hands in prayer, crying: " O God! Give Thou glory to the watchman, and riches and long life. For the watchman was Gabriel, guiding this poor one; or he was Israfil, bringing life to this wretched one !"

Indeed, his words were true, for he had found many a secret justice in this seeming tyranny of the watchman, and seen how many a mercy lay hid behind the veil. Out of wrath, the guard had led him who was athirst in love's desert to the sea of his loved one, and lit up the dark night of absence with the light of reunion.

He had driven one who was afar, into the garden of nearness, had guided an ailing soul to the heart's physician.

Now if the lover could have looked ahead, he would have blessed the watchman at the start, and prayed on his behalf, and he would have seen that tyranny as justice ; but since the end was veiled to him, he moaned and made his plaint in the beginning. Yet those who journey in the garden-land of knowledge, because they see the end in the beginning, see peace in war and friendliness in anger.

Such is the state of the wayfarers in this valley. . . .

At this hour the morn of knowledge hath arisen and the lamps of wayfaring and wandering are quenched.

> Veiled from this was Moses
> Though all strength and light ;
> Then thou who hast no wings at all,
> Attempt not flight.

If thou be a man of communion and prayer, soar up on the wings of assistance from Holy Souls, that thou mayest behold the mysteries of the Friend and attain to the lights of the Beloved. "Verily, we are from God and to Him shall we return."

After passing through the Valley of Knowledge, which is the last plane of limitation, the wayfarer cometh to THE VALLEY OF UNITY and drinketh from the cup of the Absolute, and gazeth on the Manifestations of Oneness. In this station he pierceth the veils of plurality, fleeth from the world of the flesh, and ascendeth into the heaven of singleness. With the ear of God he heareth, with the eye of God he beholdeth the mysteries of divine creation.

He sitteth on the throne of " Say, all is from God ", and taketh his rest on the carpet of " There is no power or might but in God." He looketh on all things with the eye of oneness, and seeth the brilliant rays of the divine sun shining from the dawning-point of Essence alike on all created things, and the lights of singleness reflected over all creation.

O My Brother ! A pure heart is as a mirror ; cleanse it with the burnish of love and severance from all save God, that the true sun may shine within it and the eternal morning dawn. Then wilt thou clearly see the meaning of " Neither doth My earth nor My heaven contain Me, but the heart of My faithful servant containeth Me." And thou wilt take up thy life in thine hand, and with infinite longing cast it before the new Beloved One.

Whensoever the light of Manifestation of the King of Oneness settleth upon the throne of the heart and soul, His shining becometh visible in every limb and member. At that time the mystery of the famed tradition gleameth out of the darkness : " A servant is drawn unto Me in prayer until I answer him ; and when I have answered him, I become the ear wherewith he heareth. . . ." For thus the Master of the house hath appeared within His home, and all the pillars of the dwelling are ashine with His light. And the action and effect of the light are from the Light-Giver ; so it is that all move through Him and arise by His will. And this is that spring whereof the near ones drink, as it is said. " A fount whereof the near unto God shall drink. . . ."

However, let none construe these utterances to be anthropomorphism, nor see in them the descent of the worlds of God into the grades of the creatures ; nor should they lead thy Eminence to such assumptions. For God is, in His Essence, holy above ascent and descent, entrance and exit ; He hath through all eternity been free of the attributes of human creatures, and ever will remain so. No man hath ever known Him ; no soul hath ever found the pathway to His Being. Every mystic knower hath wandered far astray in the valley of the knowledge of Him; every saint hath lost his way in seeking to comprehend His Essence. Sanctified is He above the understanding of the wise; exalted is He above the knowledge of the knowing! The way is barred and to seek it is impiety; His proof is His signs; His being is His evidence...

These mentionings that have been made of the grades of knowledge relate to the knowledge of the Manifestations of that Sun of Reality, which casteth Its light upon the Mirrors. And the splendour of that light is in the hearts, yet it is hidden under the veilings of sense and the conditions of this earth, even as a candle within a lantern of iron, and only when the lantern is removed doth the light of the candle shine out.

In like manner, when thou strippest the wrappings of illusion from off thy heart, the lights of oneness will be made manifest.

Then it is clear that even for the rays there is neither entrance nor exit—how much less for that Essence of Being and that longed-for Mystery.

Peace be upon him who concludeth this exalted journey and followeth the True One by the lights of guidance.

And the wayfarer, after traversing the high planes of this supernal journey, entereth THE VALLEY OF CONTENTMENT. In this Valley he feeleth the winds of divine contentment blowing from the plane of the spirit...

From sorrow he turneth to bliss, from anguish to joy. His grief and mourning yield to delight and rapture...

In these planes, the nightingale of the heart hath other songs and secrets, which make the heart to stir and the soul to clamour, but this mystery of inner meaning may be whispered only from heart to heart, confided only from breast to breast.

O friend, till thou enter the garden of such mysteries, thou shalt never set lip to the undying wine of this Valley. And shouldst thou taste of it, thou wilt shield thine eyes from all things else, and drink of the wine of contentment; and thou wilt loose thyself from all things else, and bind thyself to Him, and throw thy life down in His path, and cast thy soul away.

After journeying through the planes of pure contentment, the traveller cometh to THE VALLEY OF WONDERMENT and is tossed in the oceans of grandeur, and at every moment his wonder groweth. Now he seeth the shape of wealth as poverty itself, and the essence of freedom as sheer impotence. Now is he struck dumb with the beauty of the All-Glorious; again is he wearied out with his own life. How many a mystic tree hath this whirlwind of wonderment snatched by the roots, how many a soul hath it exhausted. For in this Valley the traveller is flung into confusion, albeit, in the eye of him who hath attained, such marvels are esteemed and well-beloved. At every moment he beholdeth a wondrous world, a new creation, and goeth from astonishment to astonishment, and is lost in awe at the works of the Lord of Oneness...

Likewise, reflect upon the perfection of man's creation, and that all these planes and states are folded up and hidden away within him.

> Dost thou reckon thyself only a puny form
> When within thee the universe is folded?

Then we must labour to destroy the animal condition, till the meaning of humanity shall come to light...

O friend, the heart is the dwelling of eternal mysteries, make it not the home of fleeting fancies; waste not the treasure of thy precious life in employment with this swiftly-passing world.

Thou comest from the world of holiness—bind not thine heart to the earth ; thou art a dweller in the court of nearness—choose not the homeland of the dust.

After scaling the high summits of wonderment the wayfarer cometh to THE VALLEY OF TRUE POVERTY AND ABSOLUTE NOTHINGNESS.

This station is the dying from self and the living in God, the being poor in self and rich in the Desired One. Poverty as here referred to signifieth being poor in the things of the created world, rich in the things of God's world. For when the true lover and devoted friend reacheth to the presence of the Beloved, the sparkling beauty of the Loved One and the fire of the lover's heart will kindle a blaze and burn away all veils and wrappings. Yea, all he hath, his very being, will be set aflame, so that nothing will remain save the Friend...

O My friend, listen with heart and soul to the songs of the spirit, and treasure them as thine own eyes. For the heavenly wisdoms, like the clouds of spring, will not rain down on the earth of men's hearts forever ; and though the grace of the All-Bounteous One is never stilled and never ceasing, yet to each time and era a portion is allotted and a bounty set apart, this in a given measure. "And no one thing is there, but with Us are its storehouses ; and We send it not down but in settled measure." The cloud of the Loved One's mercy raineth only on the garden of the spirit and bestoweth this bounty only in the season of spring. The other seasons have no share in this greatest grace, and barren lands no portion of this favour.

O Brother ! Not every sea hath pearls ; not every branch will flower, nor will the nightingale sing thereon. Then, ere the nightingale of the mystic paradise repair to the garden of God, and the rays of the heavenly morning return to the Sun of

Truth—make thou an effort, that haply in this dust-heap of the mortal world thou mayest catch a fragrance from the everlasting garden, and live forever in the shadow of the peoples of this city. And when thou hast attained this highest station and come to this mightiest plane, then shalt thou gaze on the Beloved, and forget all else.

> The Beloved shineth on gate and wall
> Without a veil, O men of vision.

Now hast thou abandoned the drop of life and come to the sea of the Life-Bestower. This is the goal thou didst ask for; if it be God's will, thou wilt gain it.

[*The Seven Valleys*]

D. IMMORTALITY

1. And now concerning thy question regarding the soul of man and its survival after death. Know thou of a truth that the soul, after its separation from the body, will continue to progress until it attaineth the presence of God, in a state and condition which neither the revolution of ages and centuries, nor the changes and chances of this world, can alter. It will endure as long as the Kingdom of God, His sovereignty, His dominion and power will endure. It will manifest the signs of God and His attributes, and will reveal His loving-kindness and bounty. The movement of My Pen is stilled when it attempteth to befittingly describe the loftiness and glory of so exalted a station. The honour with which the Hand of Mercy will invest the soul is such as no tongue can adequately reveal, nor any other earthly agency describe. Blessed is the soul which, at the hour of its separation from the body, is sanctified from the vain imaginings of the peoples of the world. Such a soul liveth and moveth in accord-

ance with the Will of its Creator, and entereth the all-highest Paradise. The Maids of Heaven, inmates of the loftiest mansions, will circle around it, and the Prophets of God and His chosen ones will seek its companionship. With them that soul will freely converse, and will recount unto them that which it hath been made to endure in the path of God, the Lord of all worlds. If any man be told that which hath been ordained for such a soul in the worlds of God, the Lord of the throne on high and of earth below, his whole being will instantly blaze out in his great longing to attain that most exalted, that sanctified and resplendent station . . . The nature of the soul after death can never be described, nor is it meet and permissible to reveal its whole character to the eyes of men. The Prophets and Messengers of God have been sent down for the sole purpose of guiding mankind to the straight Path of Truth. The purpose underlying their revelation hath been to educate all men, that they may, at the hour of death, ascend, in the utmost purity and sanctity and with absolute detachment, to the throne of the Most High. The light which these souls radiate is responsible for the progress of the world and the advancement of its peoples. They are like unto leaven which leaveneth the world of being, and constitute the animating force through which the arts and wonders of the world are made manifest. Through them the clouds rain their bounty upon men, and the earth bringeth forth its fruits. All things must needs have a cause, a motive power, an animating principle. These souls and symbols of detachment have provided, and will continue to provide, the supreme moving impulse in the world of being. The world beyond is as different from this world as this world is different from that of the child while still in the womb of its mother. When the soul attaineth the Presence of God, it will assume the form that best befitteth its immortality and is worthy of its celestial habitation.

Such an existence is a contingent and not an absolute existence, inasmuch as the former is preceded by a cause, whilst the latter is independent thereof. Absolute existence is strictly confined to God, exalted be His glory ...

[*Gleanings from the Writings of Bahá'u'lláh*]

2. ... Thou hast, moreover, asked Me concerning the state of the soul after its separation from the body. Know thou, of a truth, that if the soul of man hath walked in the ways of God, it will, assuredly, return and be gathered to the glory of the Beloved. By the righteousness of God! It shall attain a station such as no pen can depict, or tongue describe. The soul that hath remained faithful to the Cause of God, and stood unwaveringly firm in His Path shall, after his ascension, be possessed of such power that all the worlds which the Almighty hath created can benefit through him. Such a soul provideth, at the bidding of the Ideal King and Divine Educator, the pure leaven that leaveneth the world of being, and furnisheth the power through which the arts and wonders of the world are made manifest. Consider how meal needeth leaven to be leavened with. Those souls that are the symbols of detachment are the leaven of the world. Meditate on this, and be of the thankful.

In several of Our Tablets We have referred to this theme, and have set forth the various stages in the development of the soul. Verily I say, the human soul is exalted above all egress and regress. It is still, and yet it soareth; it moveth, and yet it is still. It is, in itself, a testimony that beareth witness to the existence of a world that is contingent, as well as to the reality of a world that hath neither beginning nor end. Behold how the dream thou hast dreamed is, after the lapse of many years, re-enacted before thine eyes. Consider how strange is the mystery of the world that appeareth to thee in thy dream. Ponder in thine heart upon the unsearchable wisdom of God, and meditate on its manifold revelations. . . .

Witness the wondrous evidences of God's handiwork, and reflect upon its range and character. He Who is the Seal of the Prophets hath said: "Increase my wonder and amazement at Thee, O God!"

[*Gleanings from the Writings of Bahá'u'lláh*]

3. Thou hast asked Me whether man, as apart from the Prophets of God and His chosen ones, will retain, after his physical death the self-same individuality, personality, consciousness, and understanding that characterize his life in this world. If this should be the case, how is it, thou hast observed, that whereas such slight injuries to his mental faculties as fainting and severe illness deprive him of his understanding and consciousness, his death, which must involve the decomposition of his body and the dissolution of its elements, is powerless to destroy that understanding and extinguish that consciousness? How can any one imagine that man's consciousness and personality will be maintained, when the very instruments necessary to their existence and function will have completely disintegrated?

Know thou that the soul of man is exalted above, and is independent of all infirmities of body or mind. That a sick person showeth signs of weakness is due to the hindrances that interpose themselves between his soul and his body, for the soul itself remaineth unaffected by any bodily ailments. Consider the light of the lamp. Though an external object may interfere with its radiance, the light itself continueth to shine with undiminished power. In like manner, every malady afflicting the body of man is an impediment that preventeth the soul from manifesting its inherent might and power. When it leaveth the body, however, it will evince such ascendancy, and reveal such influence as no force on earth can equal. Every pure, every refined and sanctified soul will be endowed with tremendous power, and shall rejoice with exceeding gladness.

Consider the lamp which is hidden under a bushel. Though its light be shining, yet its radiance is concealed from men. Likewise, consider the sun which hath been obscured by the clouds. Observe how its splendour appeareth to have diminished, when in reality the source of that light hath remained unchanged. The soul of man should be likened unto this sun, and all things on earth should be regarded as his body. So long as no external impediment interveneth between them, the body will, in its entirety, continue to reflect the light of the soul, and to be sustained by its power. As soon as, however, a veil interposeth itself between them, the brightness of that light seemeth to lessen.

Consider again the sun when it is completely hidden behind the clouds. Though the earth is still illumined with its light, yet the measure of light which it receiveth is considerably reduced. Not until the clouds have dispersed, can the sun shine again in the plenitude of its glory. Neither the presence of the cloud nor its absence can, in any way, affect the inherent splendour of the sun. The soul of man is the sun by which his body is illumined, and from which it draweth its sustenance, and should be so regarded.

Consider, moreover, how the fruit, ere it is formed, lieth potentially within the tree. Were the tree to be cut into pieces, no sign nor any part of the fruit, however small, could be detected. When it appeareth, however, it manifesteth itself, as thou hast observed, in its wondrous beauty and glorious perfection. Certain fruits, indeed, attain their fullest development only after being severed from the tree.

[*Gleanings from the Writings of Bahá'u'lláh*]

4. And now concerning thy question whether human souls continue to be conscious one of another after their separation from the body. Know thou that the souls of the people of Bahá, who have entered and been established within the Crimson Ark, shall associate and commune intimately one with another, and shall be so closely associated in their lives, their aspirations, their aims and strivings as to be even as one soul. They are indeed the ones who are well-informed, who are keen-sighted, and who are endued with understanding. Thus hath it been decreed by Him Who is the All-Knowing, the All-Wise.

The people of Bahá, who are the inmates of the Ark of God, are, one and all, well aware of one another's state and condition, and are united in the bonds of intimacy and fellowship. Such a state, however, must depend upon their faith and their conduct. They that are of the same grade and station are fully aware of one another's capacity, character, accomplishments and merits. They that are of a lower grade, however, are incapable of comprehending adequately the station, or of estimating the merits, of those that rank above them. Each shall receive his share from thy Lord. Blessed is the man that hath turned his face towards God, and walked steadfastly in His love, until his soul hath winged its flight unto God, the Sovereign Lord of all, the Most Powerful, the Ever-Forgiving, the All-Merciful.

The souls of the infidels, however, shall—and to this I bear witness—when breathing their last be made aware of the good things that have escaped them, and shall bemoan their plight, and shall humble themselves before God. They shall continue doing so after the separation of their souls from their bodies.

It is clear and evident that all men shall, after their physical death, estimate the worth of their deeds, and realize all that their hands have wrought. I swear by the Day Star that shineth above the horizon of Divine power! They that are the followers of the one true God shall, the moment they depart out of this life, experience such joy and gladness as would be impossible to describe, while they that live in error shall be seized with such fear and trembling, and shall be filled with such consternation, as nothing can exceed. Well is it with him that hath quaffed the choice and incorruptible wine of faith through the gracious favour and the manifold bounties of Him Who is the Lord of all Faiths. . . .

[*Gleanings from the Writings of Bahá'u'lláh*]

5. When we consider beings with the seeing eye, we observe that they are limited to three sorts : that is to say, as a whole, they are either mineral, vegetable, or animal ; each of these three classes containing species. Man is the highest species because he is the possessor of the perfections of all the classes ; that is, he has a body which grows and which feels. As well as having the perfections of the mineral, of the vegetable, and of the animal, he also possesses an especial excellence which the other beings are without ; that is, the intellectual perfections. Therefore man is the most noble of beings.

Man is in the highest degree of materiality, and at the beginning of spirituality ; that is to say, he is the end of imperfection and the beginning of perfection. He is at the last degree of darkness and at the beginning of light ; that is why it has been said that the condition of man is the end of the night and the beginning of day, meaning that he is the sum of all the degrees of imperfection, and that he possesses the degrees of perfection. He has the animal side as well as the angelic side ; and the aim of an educator is to so train human souls, that their angelic aspect may overcome their animal side. Then, if the divine power in man, which is his essential perfection, overcomes the satanic power, which is absolute imperfection, he becomes the most excellent among the creatures ; but if the satanic power overcomes the divine power, he becomes the lowest of the creatures. That is why he is the end of imperfection and the beginning of perfection. Not in any other of the species in the world of existence is there such a difference, contrast, contradiction, and opposition, as in the species of man. Thus the reflection of the Divine Light was in man, as in Christ, and see how loved and honoured He is ! At the same time we see man worshipping a stone, a clod of earth, or a tree : how vile he is, in that his object of worship should be the lowest existence—that is a stone, or clay, without spirit ; a mountain, a forest, or a tree. What shame is greater for man than to worship the lowest existences ? In the same way, knowledge is a quality of man, and so is ignorance ; truthfulness is a quality of man, so is falsehood ; trustworthiness and treachery, justice and injustice, are qualities of man, and so forth. Briefly, all the perfections and virtues, and all the vices, are qualities of man.

Consider equally the differences between individual men. The Christ was in the form of man, and Caiaphas was in the form of man ; Moses and Pharaoh, Abel and Cain, Bahá'u'lláh and Yaḥyá, were men.

Man is said to be the greatest representative of God, and he is the Book of Creation because all the mysteries of beings exist in him. If he comes under the shadow of the True Educator and is rightly trained, he becomes the essence of essences, the light of lights, the spirit of spirits ; he becomes the centre of the divine appearances, the source of spiritual qualities, the rising-place of heavenly lights, and the receptacle of divine inspirations. If he is deprived of this education he becomes the manifestation of satanic qualities, the sum of animal vices, and the source of all dark conditions.

The reason of the mission of the Prophets is to educate men ;

so that this piece of coal may become a diamond, and this fruitless tree may be engrafted, and yield the sweetest, most delicious fruits. When man reaches the noblest state in the world of humanity, then he can make further progress in the conditions of perfection, but not in state ; for such states are limited, but the divine perfections are endless.

Both before and after putting off this material form, there is progress in perfection, but not in state. So beings are consummated in perfect man. There is no other being higher than a perfect man. But man when he has reached this state can still make progress in perfections but not in state, because there is no state higher than that of a perfect man to which he can transfer himself. He only progresses in the state of humanity, for the human perfections are infinite. Thus, however learned a man may be, we can imagine one more learned.

Hence, as the perfections of humanity are endless, man can also make progress in perfections after leaving this world.

[*Some Answered Questions*]

BIBLIOGRAPHY

The abbreviated title used in the References is given in brackets at the end of each entry.

'Abdu'l-Bahá. *Abdul-Baha in London*. Addresses, & Notes of Conversations. Chicago : Bahai Publishing Society, 1921.
—— *The Promulgation of Universal Peace*. Discourses by Abdul Baha Abbas During His Visit to the United States in 1912. Vol. I, Chicago : Executive Board of Bahai Temple Unity, 1922. Vol. II, Chicago : Baha'i Publishing Committee, 1925. (Promulgation)
—— *The Secret of Divine Civilization*. Translated from the original Persian text by Marzieh Gail. Wilmette, Illinois : Bahá'í Publishing Trust, 1957.
—— *Some Answered Questions*. Collected and Translated from the Persian of 'Abdu'l-Bahá by Laura Clifford Barney. London : Kegan Paul, Trench, Trubner & Co. Ltd., 1908. Chicago : Bahá'í Publishing Society, 1918. London : Bahá'í Publishing Trust, 1961. Wilmette, Illinois : Bahá'í Publishing Trust, rev. edn. 1964. (Answered Questions)
—— *Tablets of 'Abdu'l-Bahá*. Vols. I, II, III, New York : Bahá'í Publishing Committee, 1909 and 1930. (Tablets)
—— Tablet to the Central Organisation for a Durable Peace, The Hague.
Bahá'u'lláh. *Gleanings from the Writings of Bahá'u'lláh*. Trans. by Shoghi Effendi. Wilmette, Illinois : Bahá'í Publishing Trust, 1935; rev. edn. 1952. London : Bahá'í Publishing Trust, 1949. (Gleanings)
—— *The Hidden Words*. Trans. by Shoghi Effendi with the assistance of some English friends. First published in England 1932. London : Bahá'í Publishing Trust, 1949. Wilmette, Illinois : Bahá'í Publishing Trust, rev. edn. 1954. (Hidden Words)

—— *The Kitáb-i-Íqán. The Book of Certitude*. Trans. by Shoghi Effendi. Wilmette, Illinois : Bahá'í Publishing Trust, 1931 ; 2nd edn. 1950. London : Bahá'í Publishing Trust, 2nd edn. 1961.

—— *Prayers and Meditations by Bahá'u'lláh*. Compiled and trans. by Shoghi Effendi. New York : Bahá'í Publishing Committee, 1938. Reprinted Wilmette, Illinois : Bahá'í Publishing Trust. London : Bahá'í Publishing Trust, 1957. (Prayers and Meditations)

—— *The Seven Valleys and The Four Valleys*. Translated by Ali-Kuli Khan (Nabílu'd-Dawlih), assisted by Marzieh Gail. Wilmette, Illinois : Bahá'í Publishing Trust, 1945 ; rev. edn. 1952. (Seven Valleys)

NABÍL-i-A'ẒAM (Muḥammad-i-Zarandí). *The Dawn-Breakers*. Nabíl's Narrative of the Early Days of the Bahá'í Revelation. Wilmette, Illinois : Bahá'í Publishing Trust, 1932. London : Bahá'í Publishing Trust, 1953.

SHOGHI EFFENDI. *The Advent of Divine Justice*. First published 1939. Wilmette, Illinois : Bahá'í Publishing Trust, rev. edn. 1963.

—— *The Promised Day Is Come*. First published 1941. Wilmette, Illinois : Bahá'í Publishing Trust, rev. edn. 1961. (Promised Day)

—— *The World Order of Bahá'u'lláh*. First published 1938. Wilmette, Illinois : Bahá'í Publishing Trust, rev. edn. 1955. (World Order)

Star of the West. The Bahá'í Magazine. Published from 1910 to 1933 from Chicago and Washington, D.C., by official Bahá'í agencies.

REFERENCES

Full details of authors and titles are given in the bibliography. Page numbers are given for both the American and British editions of *Kitáb-i-Íqán* and *The Dawn-Breakers*.

INTRODUCTION

page 2	Abdul-Baha in London, pp. 3–5.
3	Message to the London Bahá'ís on 26 November, 1911.
7–8	From a statement by Shoghi Effendi to the United Nations Special Committee on Palestine, July 1947.
8–9	World Order, pp. 103, 109.
10	World Order, p. 107.

CHAPTER I. BUILDING THE WORLD ANEW

page 12	Quotations in the second paragraph are from World Order, pp. 198, 198 and 186 respectively.
A1	Gleanings, LXX.
A2	ibid., CVI.
A3	ibid., CXII.
A4	ibid., CXIX.
A5	ibid., CXX.
A6	ibid., CVII.
A7	ibid., CXI.
A8	ibid., CX.
A9	ibid., CXVII.
B1	Promulgation, vol. I, from an address in New York, 28 May, 1912. Quotations from Promulgation have not been brought up to date as regards transliteration and capitalization.
B2	ibid., vol. II, from an address in New York, 17 November, 1912.

B3	ibid., vol. II, from the same address.
B4	Promised Day, pp. 125–6.
B5	Promulgation, vol. II, from an address in Montreal, 5 September, 1912.
B6	ibid., vol. I, from an address in New York, 1 July, 1912.
B7	ibid., vol. II, from an address in Boston, 23 July, 1912.
B8	World Order, pp. 37–8. This section from *The Secret of Divine Civilization* was retranslated by Shoghi Effendi, and quoted by him in World Order. Shoghi Effendi's translation is used in this edition.
B9	This tablet is cited in several places. It is published separately by the Bahá'í Publishing Trust, London, and it is quoted in *Foundations of World Unity*, Bahá'í Publishing Trust, Wilmette.
C1	Part of this is also quoted in the compilation *Selected Writings of 'Abdu'l-Bahá*, Bahá'í Publishing Trust, Wilmette.
C2	Promulgation, vol. II, from an address in New York, 5 December, 1912.
C3	Tablets, vol. I, pp. 40–45. A retranslation by Shoghi Effendi of the section from " O army of God ! . . ." to ". . . faithful to the covenant and Testament of God." has been substituted for the original translation. This new translation is quoted in *The Advent of Divine Justice*.
C4	Promulgation, vol. II, from an address in New York, 3 December, 1912.
C5	Star of the West, vol. V, no. 1, 21 March, 1914. Quotations from Star of the West have not been brought up to date as regards transliteration and capitalization.

CHAPTER II. GOD'S COMMAND AND EXHORTATION

A1	Gleanings, CV, part only.
A2	ibid., XCVI, part only.
A3	ibid., XLIII, part only.
A4	ibid., CIX.

A5	ibid., CXXXIX, part only.
A6	ibid., CXLVII.
A7	ibid., CLI.
A8	ibid., CLIII.
A9	ibid., CLXI, part only.
A10	ibid., CIII, part only.
B1	Hidden Words, from the Persian, no. 18.
B2	ibid., from the Persian, no. 34.
B3	ibid., from the Persian, no. 69.
B4	ibid., from the Arabic, no. 70.
B5	ibid., from the Persian, no. 76.
B6	ibid., from the Persian, Epilogue.

CHAPTER III. THE PROCLAMATION OF THE DAY OF GOD

A1	Dawn-Breakers, pp. 92-4 ; British edn. pp. 63-5.
B1	Gleanings, III, part only.
B2	ibid., IV.
B3	ibid., V.
B4	ibid., VII.
B5	ibid., X.
C1	Star of the West, vol. IV, no. 6, from a talk by 'Abdu'l-Bahá given in Paris on 3 October, 1913.
C2	ibid., vol. XIV, no. 12. A letter to the Friends in America dated 5 Safer 1314 A.H. (1896 A.D.).

CHAPTER IV. THE JOURNEY OF THE SOUL

A	GOD AND THE UNIVERSE
1	Prayers and Meditations, no. 57.
2	Answered Questions, no. 1, part only.
3	ibid., no. XLI.
B	THE PROCEEDING OF MAN FROM GOD
1	Hidden Words, from the Arabic, no. 3.
2	ibid., from the Persian, no. 29.
3	Gleanings, LXXVII, part only.

4	ibid., LXXXII, part only.
5	Answered Questions, no. LI.
6	ibid., no. LII, part only. The last paragraph is from No. L.
C	THE RETURN OF MAN TO GOD
1	Hidden Words. These six extracts are all from the Arabic, 6, 8, 9, 34, 35 and 36 respectively.
2	Kitáb-i-Íqán, pp. 192–200, part only.
3	Seven Valleys, passim.
D	IMMORTALITY
1	Gleanings, LXXXI, part only.
2	ibid., LXXXII, part only.
3	ibid., LXXX.
4	ibid., LXXXVI, part only.
5	Answered Questions, no. LXIV.